REVIEWS

"Dr Irena Yashin-Shaw's mastery is in her ability to engage on the topic of innovation in an inspirational and fun way that is also practical and meaningful. Whilst many would connect the concept of innovation with the realms of entrepreneurs, Irena brings to life in this book the role of innovators within organisations - the 'intrepreneaur'. Irena highlights the significant role that all of us can play as 'interpreneurs'- shining a light on innovation opportunities within organisations."

Amanda Yeates. General Manager.
PDO Department of Transport and Main Roads.

"I have always been impressed by how Irena uses her creative approach to develop innovations that move businesses and organisations forward. Her insight, intelligence and humour allow her to lift the scales from others' eyes so they can see new possibilities. What a bonus to have all this wisdom collected in one book."

Kevin Ryan. CEO Ryan and Associates. Author of Tilt:
Selling to today's buyers and Making Fun Work.

"Leading in the Innovation Age is an easy "must read" for leaders who want to use innovation as a key strategic theme to underpin developing better services and lower costs. Innovation leadership is about supporting your people to have the courage to make a start. This book will help you help them to do that."

Dr Lewis Atkinson. Global Partner, Haines
Centre for Strategic Management LLC.

"Dr Yashin - Shaw in *Leading in the Innovation Age* is addressing the commercial world's greatest challenge - how to win the race to the future? Her Meta Skills are a great place of focus for leaders both emerging and established. Reading her work you get a sense of calm in the chaos of change that surrounds us all. The section on *polemics, dynamics* and *mechanics* makes the implementation of change in large, complex networks viable. I loved it, well written, easy to read and practical."

Matt Church. Founder Thought Leaders Global.
Author of 'Amplifiers: The power of motivational
leadership to inspire and influence.'

"The genius of *Leading in the Innovation Age* is its beguiling simplicity. Irena's book gently, but firmly, strips away any notion that innovation is a 'someday' proposition in our organisations. It challenges our belief that innovative work is only done by entrepreneurs, in startups or by techno-geeks. Instead, Irena reveals how everyday people - cubicle commandos in the Australian public and private sectors, small business, education and not- for-profits - are the secret sauce of innovation. Her book shows that, by supporting our people to build seven innovation meta-skills, our work will be competitive and commended in the Innovation Age."

Dr. Emily Verstege. Founder, Multiplicite. Author of 'Getting to
Awesome: A manifesto for building great stuff that people love to use'

"The future is here! If you don't get on board, or you don't know how, you will become irrelevant. This book shows us how to develop the skills we need to thrive in the Innovation Age. Throughout this exceptional book, Irena gives us practical tips on *how* to push ourselves into a space of true leadership. She shows us the simple developments that we can and should undertake if we want an innovative workplace. An easy read that demonstrates exactly why Dr Yashin-Shaw is a leader of leaders."

Dr. Amy Silver. Leadership and high performance expert.

"In an uncertain and dramatically changing future, innovative practice will no longer be considered an optional extra. It will become a mandatory requirement, and the talented Dr Irena Yashin-Shaw is the one who can help you to implement this much-needed thinking for the future. If you are serious about innovation, then read this book. Her 'Meta-Skills' will make a profound difference to the professional world."

Tony Ryan. Educator and Futurist. Author of 'The Ripple Effect' and the 'Thinkers Keys'.

"More than anyone else I know, Irena has a natural ability to empower, inspire and believe in each person's potential. In workshops, I have seen the effortless way that Irena makes innovation accessible and am delighted that she has successfully translated that freshness into print. In a world of innovation-induced fear and anxiety, Irena has produced THE self-help guide to not only navigate change but lead it and reap the benefits."

Paul Hodgson. Economic Development Manager. Ipswich City Council.

LEADING
IN THE
INNOVATION AGE

LEADING

IN THE

INNOVATION AGE

Unleash knowledge, talent and experience to
create an innovative workplace

Dr. Irena Yashin-Shaw

Irena Yashin-Shaw
PO Box 65, Mansfield LPO, Mansfield,
Brisbane, QLD, 4122
+61 7 3849 5003
irena@innovationedge.com.au
www.innovationedge.com.au

Limits of Liability and Disclaimer of Warranty
The author and publisher shall not be liable for your misuse of this material. This book is strictly for informational and educational purposes.

Warning – Disclaimer
The purpose of this book is to educate and entertain. The author and/ or publisher do not guarantee that anyone following these techniques, suggestions, tips, ideas or strategies will become successful. The author and/or publisher shall have neither liability nor responsibility to anyone with respect to any loss or damage caused, or alleged to be caused, directly or indirectly by the information contained in this book.

ISBN: 978-0-9954120-0-2   eISBN: 978-0-9954120-1-9

ACKNOWLEDGEMENTS

It is always a pleasure to give gratitude.

Thanks to all the wonderful leaders I have worked with around the world and in so many different contexts. Although I have usually been the one with the title of teacher, trainer or mentor, there is no doubt in my mind that I have learnt more from all of you than you have from me. In particular, I want to acknowledge the amazing business leaders and public sector leaders who have come through my *Innovative Leaders Mentoring Program*. Without exception, you have inspired me. It has been a privilege to share in your journeys.

Thanks and acknowledgements to Anthea Horvat, a very talented business coach who brought valuable insights to my business model.

To the *Thought Leaders Community*. It is a privilege to belong to and journey with such an exceptional group of people.

Gratitude goes to Tania Heyblom, my executive manager who keeps my business running and keeps me organised.

Special love to my gorgeous mum, Merle, for her lifelong support, unconditional love and unwavering belief in me and every undertaking I have ever turned my hand to.

And finally, my wonderful husband, Phil, and beautiful daughter, Illariya, who are the bedrock of my life. You make it all possible and worthwhile.

Leaders at all levels seeking to inspire, lead and embed innovation in their teams and workplaces have a powerful resource and ally in Dr Irena Yashin-Shaw. She understands the challenges leaders face when wanting to create innovative, creative, high-performing workplaces that are adaptable in fast-moving times.

Irena works with smart, forward-thinking leaders who want to unleash the knowledge, talent and experience within their people. Her programs cultivate leaders for the innovation age so they can create innovation-enabled, future-focussed, vibrant workplaces.

Working across all sectors, public, corporate, business and education, Irena has, inspired, mentored and trained thousands of leaders globally to become more innovative. Complementing her hands-on experience, Irena has the formal academic credentials that ensure her depth of knowledge. These include a PhD in creativity, Master of Adult Education, Bachelor of Arts, a teaching degree and communication qualifications from Trinity College London. She is also a Fellow of the Australian Institute of Management and is a Certified Speaking Professional, an award bestowed only on professional speakers of the highest caliber (there are fewer than 600 CSPs globally).

Irena lives in Brisbane, Australia, but travels nationally and internationally to deliver keynote presentations, workshops and consultations.

PREFACE

With all the books about leadership currently in print, do we really need another one? Yes, we do. No other leadership book pulls together leadership concepts in the way presented here. This book is a powerful encapsulation of a variety of essential messages, summarised in an acronym which also delivers its own meaning. It is an indispensable tool for leaders looking for simple frameworks for complex workplaces and workplace issues.

This book has been designed with simplicity in mind: the length, layout and language. My hope is that you find it easy to read; that it is easy to pick up and put down in the small slivers of time you have between activities as you shift gears. I have worked with enough leaders to know that the greatest gift is a high-value return for a low investment of time and energy. It is one of the characteristics of the innovation age.

In each chapter, I share stories and research gained from my own first-hand experience working as a corporate educator and innovation mentor. I also share examples from the public domain, as well as academic research. Names and personal information have been changed in the first-hand stories I share.

Many of the case studies and illustrative examples come from public-sector contexts. This is where the bulk of my work has concentrated for the past few years. However, the lessons learnt from them are relevant to *any sector*.

This book is not about *organisational* redesign; it's about *leadership* redesign. It is leadership that creates culture, so we will start with that. The focus of this book is how innovative leaders think, act and inspire people in the innovation age to create an innovative workplace.

As you read, you may form ideas about how you can implement some of the concepts and tips. There is a notes page at the end of every chapter so you can capture your brilliant thoughts immediately.

CONTENTS

WELCOME TO THE INNOVATION AGE

"Innovation is the only insurance against irrelevance."

~ Gary Hamel

CHAPTER 1

Welcome to the Innovation Age

"If the rate of change on the outside exceeds the
rate of change on the inside, the end is near."
~ Jack Welch

We live in the most remarkable time in history. The world is transforming itself before our eyes. It is our "second renaissance".

As in the first renaissance of the 15th and 16th centuries, knowledge and creativity are highly marketable commodities used to fuel business, commerce and profit. The sudden spread of information made possible by the invention of Johannes Gutenberg's printing press in 1440 caused an explosion of scientific creativity in Europe. Information became more accessible and easier to build upon. The same thing happened in the late '90s when the internet became mainstream. Suddenly, people had access to vast amounts of information – and it was free, for the most part. They could connect with people around the world and collaborate with ease.

It has been innovation and creativity, rather than productivity, that have produced such an enormous acceleration in the pace of change. New technologies, ideas and products generate their own markets, thereby eliminating the danger of market saturation. The global economic infrastructure can now support and exploit the explosion of new ideas and technologies. New knowledge finances and provides a platform for further knowledge creation, and highly skilled workers are substantially rewarded for generating new and innovative ideas, commodities and technologies.

Welcome to the innovation age.

It is an era of disruptive business models such as Uber, Airbnb, Couchsurfing, Fiverr, TaskRabbit and Upwork, which bypass traditional service channels to directly connect customers with providers. Increasingly, we are going to see the "uberisation" (there's a word that would have had no meaning a few years ago) of all sorts of activities, not just the obvious ones of meal and grocery delivery.

Healthcare, transport, manufacturing and even fashion will soon be disrupted by the internet of things (IoT), self-driving cars, 3D printing and wearable computing.

Over the next 10 – 15 years, 40% of jobs will be lost to automation.[1] By 2020, technical knowledge will double at the rate of every 73 days.[2] That may have seemed incomprehensible even a few years ago but completely believable in an era of artificial intelligence, virtual reality, augmented reality, drones, advanced robotics, 3D printing, 4D printing[3], IoT, quantum computing, cloud computing, autonomous vehicles, commercial space flights, gene editing, nanotechnology, biotechnology and renewable energy.

We are on an exponential change curve when it comes to technological knowledge creation. Extrapolating from this curve, by the end of this century, we would not have experienced merely 100 years of progress – it will be more like 20,000 years of development. Twenty thousand years ago, Cro-Magnon man was hunting deer with spears in the last ice age. We cannot even begin to imagine what our grandchildren will be doing in 2099, but they will be as far removed from us technologically as we are now from Cro-Magnon man. Our latest technologies will look like the equivalent of a spear to them!

More than 90% of information in the world today was created in the past two years. Every 60 seconds, 13,000 mobile apps are downloaded, 695,000 searches are made on Google and 510,000 comments are made on Facebook.

Fortune 500 companies, whose global positioning once looked secure and unassailable, are losing market share, or worse – going out of business completely. The average lifespan of a large organisation has shrunk from about 70 years in the mid-20th century to about 15 years (and dropping).[4] That means only 16% of companies started today will survive beyond one generation. At the other end of the spectrum, 70% of the companies that will be household names in 2020 haven't even been heard of yet.

Think about how quickly companies can burst onto the scene, seemingly out of nowhere. For example, Uber went from net worth $0 to $18 billion in five years.

It is indisputable that we are living in an exponential world. It stands to reason that organisations travelling at a linear pace in an exponential world are going to fall into the *Innovation Gap*. Keeping up is the new standing still.

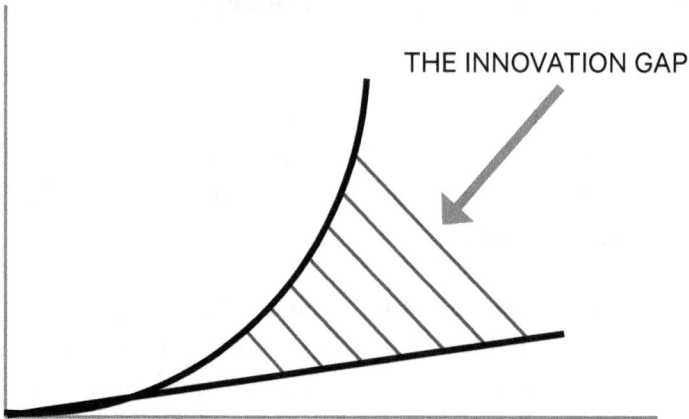

THE INNOVATION GAP

Awaiting you in the innovation gap are bankruptcy and dissatisfied clients. Obsolescence. Irrelevance!

In my keynote presentations and workshops, I ask people if they can think of organisations that have fallen into the innovation gap. The first example that comes to people's minds is Kodak. When it invented the digital camera in the mid- '70s, Kodak had the means to take a leap forward and secure its future market position.

The digital camera was a brilliant breakthrough and one that should have made Kodak the market leader of the digital age. Instead, the digital camera became the means of its own destruction because Kodak didn't see the potential. Kodak chose to hold onto its global dominance in the print-based photography space. Its reasoning was, "If we are the best in the world at this, we'll be fine." Kodak held off commercialising its digital invention for fear of hurting or cannibalising its print-based business. It didn't consider the possibility that the world may no longer want what it was the best at producing. As far as bad calls go, this was staggering.

The yawning jaws of the innovation gap swallowed Kodak in 2012. After being around for 120 years and employing 50,000 people worldwide, Kodak filed for bankruptcy. It is a cautionary tale of what can happen in the absence of imagination and visionary leadership. Sadly, Kodak is not an isolated example. Over the past decade, many high-profile organisations have succumbed to the innovation gap: Blackberry, Blockbuster, Borders. You can probably think of many more.

This raises the following question: In a world changing so rapidly, *what new skills do leaders need to ensure the success of their organisations?*

The 2016 World Economic Forum report *The Future of Jobs: Employment, Skills and Workforce Strategy for the Fourth Industrial Revolution*[5] suggests that by 2020, "more than a third of the desired core skill sets of most occupations will be comprised of skills that are not yet considered crucial to the job today." So-called *soft skills* – in particular, social skills such as emotional intelligence and teaching others – "will be in higher demand across industries than narrow technical skills, such as programming or equipment operation and control. In essence, technical skills will need to be supplemented with strong social and collaboration skills."

This vital new skill set for leaders is the subject of this book, and what I refer to as meta-skills. I will explain why I use this term shortly. But first, let us examine in more detail the way the world has changed.

What shifts have taken place in the qualities that are most highly prized and rewarded in leaders?

What qualities are valued in workplaces now compared to 10 or even five years ago?

Metaphorically speaking, the environments of contemporary workplaces are like the moveable infrastructure of Hogwarts in the world of *Harry Potter*. Staircases shift, walls slide, corridors change direction. How do we navigate in such shifting circumstances? Are our schools and universities preparing the new crop of workplace recruits to be nimble?

One thing is for sure, we can't prepare for a fluid future by looking to the past. Looking at what worked yesterday will not prepare us for tomorrow. In the next chapter, we look at why this is.

NOTES

_____

_____

_____

_____

_____

_____

_____

_____

_____

_____

_____

_____

_____

_____

_____

_____

_____

WHAT'S DIFFERENT

"Progress is impossible without change, and those who
cannot change their minds cannot change anything."
~ George Bernard Shaw

CHAPTER 2

What's Different

"Change is the law of life. And those who look only to
the past or present are certain to miss the future."

~ John F. Kennedy

In this chapter, we will look at how our thinking about the kinds of behaviours that are most useful in the workplace has changed. A number of these concepts will be explored more deeply in later chapters.

Each year, GE produces a *Global Innovation Barometer,* which reports on global research findings and insights. GE interviews senior executives from around the world to study the drivers and deterrents of innovation. In 2013, GE interviewed more than 3000 leaders in 25 countries. The 2013 report[6] found that *"education, development and access to talent was a critical concern for innovation leaders. The creativity and technical prowess of the global workforce is seen as key to unlocking innovation potential across companies and countries. But concerns around the preparedness of the workforce to innovate for tomorrow's economy abound."* In other words, while there is an acknowledged need for talented, skilled, creative people to drive innovation in the future, the current workforce is ill-equipped to do so.

Three years down the track, the 2016 GE *Global Innovation Barometer*[7] shows that problem-solving skills and creativity (beyond the necessary technical qualifications for a job) are now the top two most highly desired workplace skills globally. Yet only a few countries (Australia is not one of them) feel that their education system has adapted sufficiently to meet the demand for the new talent and skills required in the innovation age.

Why is this so? And what can we do about it? In exploring answers to these questions, allow me tell you a little about my own journey, which will help shed some light on why we have this situation.

I started my work life as a high-school teacher. As a beginning mathematics and science teacher more than 30 years ago, I was well versed in the values of a 20th-century Western education system. I was an excellent example of both the product and the propagator of the thinking that had made the second half of the 20th century the age of the knowledge worker operating in the knowledge economy.

It was an era so called because of the unprecedented number of people who made their living by applying academic knowledge acquired in school and university rather than through manual labor.

It was an era that valued and rewarded logical, analytical and critical thinking skills above creativity and imagination. Many out-of-the-box thinkers did not flourish in such a system. Sir Ken Robinson, the crusader of creativity in schools, points out: "Many highly talented, brilliant, creative people think they're not – because the thing they were good at school wasn't valued, or was actually stigmatised.[9]"

When I was at school, there was an unwritten expectation that if you did well academically in junior high school, then you should go on to do physics, chemistry, maths B and maths C in senior high school. They were disciplines that prepared you well for highly analytical courses at university: the types that usually focused on getting the right answers by applying the right process, being able to memorise complex formulae and knowing when to use them.

I emerged as a maths and science teacher ready to continue this great educational tradition, which relegated creative pursuits to the "poor cousins" of the academic world because of the perceived lack of mental discipline they required.

How ironic that later, I went on to do a PhD in creativity. In hindsight, I believe the reason for that was because my creative capacities, which had been stifled for so long, demanded to be rediscovered and recognised. It became too uncomfortable to neglect them. And thus began my subsequent quest to understand the creative process and how we can develop that side of ourselves.

The model for understanding and developing creative thinking skills, which I developed during my research, takes a "whole brain" approach to problem solving. It is in recognition of the fact that analytical thought alone serves a purpose, but is not sufficient for the new age in which we live today: the innovation age. It is an era that requires successful leaders to be able to effectively integrate different kinds of thinking – creative and logical thought processes, imagination with analysis, and generative thinking with critical thinking.

Today, we have unprecedented access to information. Anyone with internet access an obtain vast stores of information at the click of a button or the touch of a screen. However, simply having plenty of knowledge or access to information is no guarantee that it will be used well.

My old school motto was *Scientia Est Potestas*. Knowledge is Power. It is a saying that grew out of a bygone time when knowledge was hard to come by. The only people who had access to knowledge were the wealthy or the clergy. It is completely outdated in a world where we have a glut of information; where knowledge, on its own, has lost its currency.

Today, the "power" is in being able to transform that knowledge. It is in being able to synthesise, synergise and shape that knowledge in new ways and for new purposes; to solve new problems and to look at old problems in new ways.

My old school should change its motto to Innovation is Power. *Innovatus Est Potestus*. (I haven't suggested it as I don't think it would be well received.)

This is exactly what we are seeing globally. Organisations, leaders and individuals who innovate effectively do well. Those who don't fall into the innovation gap.

The Shift

Let's identify some specific ways in which the world has changed and how our thinking needs to change to create the kind of workforce that is innovation ready.

On the following page is a set of five words that characterise qualities that traditionally have been highly valued – in the world of education as well as work. Can you think of a corresponding set of words that represent the new qualities that have become important to contemporary education and workplaces?

This is not to say these qualities are without value; simply that in a volatile and fast-changing world, they do not serve us as well as they did in the past. We need to evolve and augment this kind of thinking if we are to have a hope of being successful in the innovation age.

Right answers   ➡   ?

Individual work   ➡   ?

Conformity   ➡   ?

Control   ➡   ?

Linear thinking   ➡   ?

There are no standard answers. This is an exercise to get you thinking. It is a great discussion starter for a team meeting. You may come up with a set of words or concepts completely different to those I explore in the next few pages.

From Right Answers Towards Right Questions

Right answers are still important, of course. But we can find right answers from a simple Google search. Today, it is equally as important to ask the *right questions*. At a time when organisations need to challenge the status quo to move forward quickly, the right questions help challenge entrenched thinking and identify opportunities.

Questions are the new answers! If we want better outcomes, we need to ask better questions.

If we don't ask questions, we end up with "group think". This is a pattern of agreement where no one questions ideas, policies or actions. As American journalist and author Walter Lippmann said, "Where all think alike, no-one thinks very much." And that is dangerous! There are many examples of leaders making dreadful blunders and poor decisions when they don't ask the right questions at the right time.

The Titanic disaster is one example. More than 1400 people tragically lost their lives in the icy waters of the North Atlantic Ocean in April 1912. During the investigation that followed, it was discovered that some of the ship's planners and builders had been concerned about a number of issues. Unfortunately, they never raised their concerns in the company of their peers for fear of appearing foolish. They thought that if no other "expert" was unsure about the structure and safety of the ship, everything must be OK.

I remember watching in horror on January 28, 1986, as so many of us did, when the space shuttle Challenger exploded 73 seconds into its flight. Later, it came to light there had been serious concerns about the reliability of the O-ring, a sealing component that prevented hot gasses escaping. But when the time came to ask questions, the people who should have didn't.

If we were to analyse man-made disasters, we would find that most would have lacked an intelligent, independent asking of questions beforehand.

Dr Robert Cialdini, best-selling author and Professor Emeritus of Psychology and Marketing at Arizona State University, devotes a whole chapter to "social proof" in his landmark book, *Influence: The Psychology of Persuasion*[8]. Social proof influences people to unquestioningly go along with things they see other people go along with. It is a phenomenon pervasive across organisations, and leaders need to guard against it. And you can – by asking questions. Good ones.

Nurturing a "question-asking" mentality among team members makes them – and the organisation as a whole – responsive to change. They will become adaptable and innovative. And that is vital to success in the innovation age, where yesterday's solutions won't solve tomorrow's problems.

Questions compel us to challenge the relevance of our established mental models. It allows us to recalibrate them when necessary. Asking good questions helps people keep their thinking fresh, their outcomes innovative and their careers moving forward.

As Peter Drucker, celebrated guru of management theory and practice, said: "The leader of the past was the person who told. The leader of the future is the person who *asks*."

From Individual Work Towards Collaborative Work

In this hyper-connected world, it has never been easier to collaborate as part of a team. And if two heads are better than one, then many heads are better than two. Technology has given us countless collaboration platforms: Wikis, Google Docs, SharePoint, Yammer, Facebook and many others. It's a long list.

When English poet John Donne penned his famous words, "No man is an island entire of itself; every man is a piece of the continent, a part of the main," nearly 400 years ago, little could he have imagined how prophetic they were. His words are relevant more than ever in our constantly connected, globalised community.

Collaboration accelerates outcomes and delivers better results because it facilitates the synthesis of diverse skill sets. It brings different perspectives and a broader knowledge base to the table when solving problems.

In the past, it was not unusual for people to hoard information because knowledge was power. And, unfortunately, some people still cling to this mindset, which can cause problems for teams. Sometimes, hoarding is unintentional. It's what people are used to: they haven't learnt the new way of collaborating yet. Henning Kagermann, former CEO of German software corporation SAP, said: "We have learned that *sharing* knowledge is the best way to *get* knowledge. If you feel you have to protect yourself, you have already lost half of the game."[10]

From Conformity Towards Creativity

The world has always had non-conformists, but historically they haven't been well rewarded. People who toed the "party" line and didn't question authority were likely to be rewarded, rather than those who had out-of-the box, original or radical ideas.

For most of human history, people who had ideas that were genuinely novel, that presented people with a different view of the world, were likely to meet a premature and often unpleasant end. Greek philosopher Socrates, whose philosophies challenged the status quo, was forced to drink hemlock. Italian scientist and philosopher Galileo Galilei lived out the end of his life under house arrest and was refused visitors because of his assertion that the Earth and planets revolved around the sun. French heroine Joan of Arc was burnt at the stake. The popular belief was she was burned for practising witchcraft, but in fact one of the main cases against her was dressing like a man. History is full of people who have paid a high price for being non-conformists.

But today, we recognise that conformity breeds complacency. And complacency leads to irrelevance, which is a surefire route into the innovation gap. Progressive organisations encourage rather than discourage their people to come up with new ideas and ensure their voices are heard.

There is a global awakening to the fact that creativity can be an everyday activity. It is not something exclusive to geniuses who produce paradigm-shifting breakthroughs. I will explore this topic in more detail in Chapter 6.

From Control Towards Flexibility

Workplaces are moving away from highly defined, rigid work arrangements and organisational structures. They acknowledge that highly controlled environments can stifle creativity and innovation. Authoritarian leadership practices that result in the micro-management of employees can cause gross inefficiencies, loss of productivity and bottlenecks.

A culture of control and corporate hierarchy in the organisational structure of Kodak was partly responsible for its demise. Much has been written about the fall of the photography giant (hindsight is a great vantage point). A key factor was that it was unable to change a culture left over from an earlier manufacturing age, where staff didn't question leaders' decisions or challenge the status quo.

Ceding control on the part of a leader is not a sign of weakness; rather, it signals trust in team members. If team members are not ready to have some control, then they need to be developed.

From Linear Thinking Towards Design Thinking

How many of us have been in a meeting or a series of meetings, where we have been tasked with solving a particular workplace problem, come up with a solution, developed a sequentially stepped action plan and gone off to apply it?

On the surface, it sounds like an efficient way of proceeding. Except that in a fast-moving, complex world, there is every chance that by the time you apply the solution to the original problem, things have changed and you could be solving the wrong problem.

Design thinking uses an iterative, incremental approach to problem-solving that is flexible. The solution is built up and created *en route* (so to speak), incorporating new information as it emerges and becomes relevant. This is then synthesised into the emerging solution.

For example, when I do organisational transformation work, I constantly re-design and re-engineer how things will play out. Taking people through an innovation process is a complex activity. There are numerous moving parts. People respond differently in different situations. Priorities change, and new information comes to light. This can spark unforeseen reactions; timeframes can become slippery.

It's dangerous to come in with a prescriptive solution and set approach. Although we know roughly what the end game looks like, the steps to get us there are constantly being recalibrated. That's a design-thinking approach.

Our VUCA World

This 21st-century world, with its new operating manual, has come to be known as a VUCA world.

The acronym VUCA was originally coined by the US defence department to describe the post-Cold War global landscape from a military perspective. It stands for **Volatile Uncertain Complex Ambiguous**. While the term describes a chaotic, destabilised world following the fall of communism, it has also found its way into "organisational speak". VUCA reflects the need for modern workplaces to adapt quickly to the changing demands of innovation-hungry clients and new technological developments.

No sector, whether public, private, education or not-for-profit, is exempt for the impact of a rapidly changing world. Without VUCA-enabled leaders, an organisation will flounder.

Research conducted by global consulting firm DDI – and reported in its *Global Leadership Forecast* 2014/2015[11] – showed that the

VUCA capability of leaders was directly linked to an organisation's financial performance. "The top 20% of organisations performing well financially are three times more likely to have VUCA-capable leaders than the bottom 20%."

Kevin Roberts, previously global CEO and briefly chairman of Saatchi & Saatchi, one of the world's leading creative organisations, went so far as to say we live in a *super*-VUCA world. But Roberts' VUCA stands for **V**ibrant **U**nreal **C**razy **A**stounding. Roberts is an inspirational leadership speaker and I had the opportunity to meet him a couple of years ago when he spoke at a conference in Sydney. I liked his spin on VUCA. I'll forgive him for putting it on steroids and "super-fying" it – he is in marketing, after all.

Ironically, Roberts now understands only too well the dangers of a VUCA world, where *nothing* can be taken for granted. After an illustrious 40-year career working for some of the world's best-known brands, he was forced to resign after his controversial statement that the "debate is over when it comes to diversity in his industry". Seems Roberts had his own "Kodak moment". Or perhaps he will live by his own mantra, "fail fast, fix fast, learn fast", and reinvent himself.

VUCA is the new normal. Some might find that exhilarating, others horrifying. Either way, we need to update the way we think, problem solve and lead.

A wonderful metaphor for how to do things differently to succeed in a VUCA world is provided by Patrick Hollingworth in his book, *The Light and Fast Organisation* (2016)[12]. An avid mountain climber, Hollingworth describes the difference between two very different styles of climbing to represent different ways of leading.

The expedition style of climbing is heavy going. The climber expects the journey to the summit to take a long time, and to be arduous and dangerous, so sets off with all the equipment needed for survival. It makes for a slow-going climb.

The alpinist, on the other hand, also understands that the journey to the summit will be arduous and dangerous, but sets off with just a few essential items. This climber's plan is to reach the summit quickly and return before nightfall. The alpinist succeeds by travelling light and fast.

The statistics show that more people are killed by expedition-style mountaineering than by alpine style. The message to organisations and leaders is this: adopt an alpine approach. Be light and fast; you'll have fewer casualties. I hope this book provides you with insight into how to achieve this.

Now, it's possible, even likely, that someone reading this is saying to themselves, "I work in government. Bureaucracies R Us! How can we do light and fast?"

The pressure on government agencies to reinvent themselves has never been greater. The Australian Public Service Commission, in its 2015 document *Unlocking Potential*[13], says: "Workforce practices must be flexible enough to allow agencies to continually challenge talented employees and respond quickly to changing business priorities."

Sure, it's easy to write that in a document, but it's much harder to do. And in Australia, we've seen calls like this consistently over the past several years.

In 2010, the Australian Public Service Commission's document *Empowering Change – Fostering Change in the APS*[14] opened with the statement: "Innovation is at the heart of good public administration." In 2013, the NSW Public Service Commission published its *Ideas at Work: Creating an Innovative Public Sector*[15] manifesto, in which it recognised its key role was to "assist by identifying the organisational conditions that foster creative, solutions-focused thinking and support for emerging good ideas." In Queensland, networks such as the Business Innovation and Improvement in Government Network bring world-class innovation training, education and ideas to agencies across the state. At a federal level, the Public Sector Innovation Network has produced a comprehensive innovation toolkit.[16]

But the question is, are all these calls and initiatives bringing about the desired outcomes? Is innovation getting traction in the public sector?

Yes.

The public sector in Australia is innovating! This is despite all kinds of legacy frameworks and outdated procedures and systems. Dedicated public servants with a passion to create a better society are innovating. As someone who works extensively across the public sector, I see first-hand the fast-growing appetite for innovation across all levels of government. But there's much more evidence than my observations to substantiate this claim.

Recently, Professor Peter Gahan at the University of Melbourne and his team from the Centre for Workplace Leadership released the findings of a landmark study called *Leadership at Work: Do Australian leaders have what it takes?*[17] On page 75, you will find this stunning statement: "Public organisations are more innovative than private ones. A significantly smaller proportion of private organisations and a significantly larger proportion of public organisations are among high performers on radical innovation."

Now, that has to give us pause! It seems that alpine style is gaining traction in the public sector after all.

Meta-Skills for the Innovation Age

It is a leader's responsibility to show people that the world has radically shifted and to keep doing things the established way is dangerous. Innovation is the new safety net and the riskiest course of action is to *not* innovate.

The next few years will make unprecedented demands on our courage, imagination and leadership skills. Leaders must be prepared with a new skill set that is above and beyond what they have needed previously. It is a skill set transferable to any context, work environment or team.

The prefix "meta" means beyond. It implies a concept that is an abstraction from another concept. I've called this new set of skills "meta-skills" because they are the catalysing agents that optimise, galvanise and capitalise on other, more specific, skills. Furthermore, they are leadership skills that can be put into any context. They are the skills that will help leaders create innovative workplaces.

The progression goes like this. As leaders, at the core of our expertise are the technical skills and job-specific skills that we started out with in our careers. Over time, through experience, training and development, we deepen, widen and sometimes change these skill sets altogether.

Inevitably, as we develop in our roles, grow into various responsibilities, change jobs, head teams, manage projects and attend training sessions, we acquire self-leadership skills that help us improve our productivity, better manage our time and use technology tools for various purposes. We also learn, either formally through a program or informally by trial and error, the fundamentals of leading others: negotiation, communication, presentation and emotional intelligence. You fill out the list from your experience. We'll call these "foundational leadership skills".

And yes, I'm simplifying it: personal and professional development doesn't happen sequentially, but you get the picture.

What I'm leading up to is that all these skills – technical skills and foundational leadership skills – are extremely useful for leaders and aspiring leaders, but they are not *enough* in the innovation age. To lead innovation and to lead *for* innovation, we need a new *meta-skill* set.

Let's use the layers of the Earth as a metaphor.

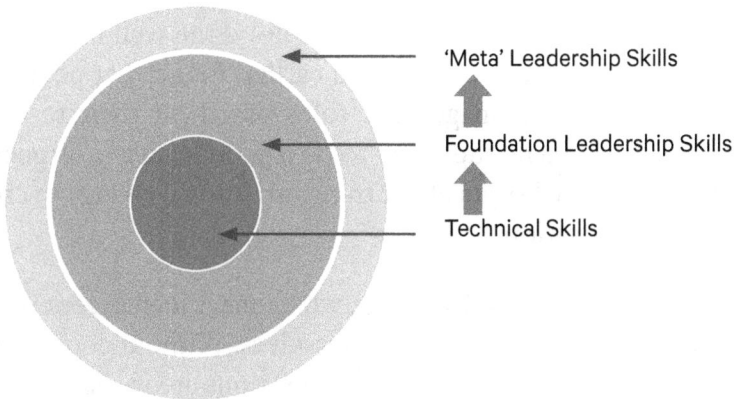

'Meta' Leadership Skills

Foundation Leadership Skills

Technical Skills

The solid inner core is made of iron and forms the foundation of the Earth's existence. These are our core technical skills – an essential foundation. Usually, the starting point of our career.

Surrounding the core is a molten layer that spins, generating the all-important magnetic fields of the Earth on which life depends. These are the foundational leadership skills we acquire as we progress through our professional practice.

But it is the outer layer of the Earth's mantle where all the exciting action takes place. This is where diversity flourishes and multiple complex, adaptive systems intersect and interact, producing the myriad forms of life in all their glory. This represents the innovation layer. This is the skill set leaders need to motivate, energise, guide and develop their teams to create dynamic, future- ready, innovative workplaces.

To continue the metaphor, the top layer is also the thinnest and most fragile. Leaders who aspire to drive innovation can be vulnerable. They challenge the status quo, take risks and shake things up. Consequently, they can become easy targets if they are not supported in their efforts.

Considerable research shows that the development leaders must undergo in order to lead innovation is not done well in Australia. The *Leadership at Work* study, cited earlier, found that people are often promoted to management roles based on their technical skills, yet they have no idea how to be a good leader[18] – especially the kind of leader who can effect transformational change to create a culture of innovation.

This situation is not new. However, what makes it an urgent issue is the new context in which we find ourselves. Without good leaders at all levels in our VUCA world, organisations are in danger! They won't simply be poor performers; much worse – they'll become irrelevant. And then, it's a small step to extinction.

In this book, I identify and unpack seven of these meta-skills that will help leaders to be more effective in their leadership roles in the innovation age. You'll see later why I have chosen these *particular* words to describe these skills.

NOTES

_____

_____

_____

_____

_____

_____

_____

_____

_____

_____

_____

_____

_____

_____

_____

_____

_____

META-SKILL # 1
ENTREPRENEURIALISM

"Do not be embarrassed by your failures,
learn from them and start again."

~ Richard Branson

CHAPTER 3

Meta-Skill #1 Entrepreneurialism

"The skills of an entrepreneur are the skills of the 21st-century worker."
~ Queen Rania of Jordan

When we think of an entrepreneur, we usually think of someone like Richard Branson. Someone who has fearlessly and boldly taken risks to build a massive global empire. Indeed, entrepreneurs are people who conduct their business innovatively. They create opportunities that didn't previously exist and seek to multiply the investment of their time and resources.

But are such endeavours exclusively the domain of the Richard Bransons of the world?

Everyone can be an entrepreneur

I believe that anyone, in any workplace, who seeks to be opportunistic and resourceful, who adds value and solves problems, who constantly searches for ways to create opportunities is entrepreneurial.

Such people work in large and small businesses, schools and universities, government agencies, not-for-profit companies and charitable organisations. In short, entrepreneurs exist *everywhere*. And it is a skill we can all demonstrate.

I love the quote at the beginning of this chapter by Queen Rania of Jordan. I came across it in a newspaper article when I was in Amman, the capital of Jordan. I was there to deliver a keynote presentation at a large public-sector innovation conference for the Middle East region. As part of my final preparations the night before the conference, I scoured the local newspapers to see what issues were topical. I always look for current local content to include in my presentations.

It just so happened that the World Economic Forum had held a conference in Amman the week before, and Queen Rania had delivered the opening address. One of the local English language newspapers had printed her speech word for word. As I read it, I was struck by her key messages, which resonated with the key messages I was to deliver in my speech the next morning. So I quoted her that day (which was very well received) and have continued to quote her ever since. There is powerful wisdom in that one sentence. "The skills of an entrepreneur are the skills of the 21st-century worker."

Anytime someone experiences a disappointing result and asks themselves, "Where is the *opportunity* in this?", they are being entrepreneurial. When they depart from the status quo in order to provide a better customer experience or serve the community more effectively, they are being entrepreneurial.

Entrepreneurialism is an attitude of resilience that sees the potential and possibility in situations others may consider failures, whether they are a business owner, an engineer or a scientist.

The famous story of 3M's Post-it® notes is an example of this. In 1968, 3M scientist Spencer Silver was trying to create a super-strong adhesive, but was disappointed with its performance. It was considered too weak to be useful. However, years later, chemical engineer and 3M product development engineer Art Fry discovered the low-tack adhesive was perfect for temporary attachment to documents. Had a less entrepreneurial engineer been working at 3M, we might never have had Post-it® notes.

To be entrepreneurial means to be consciously focused on rewards rather than the fear of loss. Fear is a much more powerful motivator than reward. This is why some people don't take risks. They are too afraid of what they might lose, which eclipses the joy and benefits they might gain. We have to change the mindset of "if it ain't broke, don't fix it" to "fix things *before* they get broken".

To create an entrepreneurial workplace where opportunities are identified and exploited, research shows that the primary factor is leaders who act as role models.[19] Other factors are team members' level of empowerment and the level of environmental support through resources.

Risk Taking

Risk strikes fear in the hearts of some leaders – especially those who consider themselves to work in severely risk-averse contexts. However, taking a risk is not necessarily about being irresponsible, naive or reckless. Calculated risks require due diligence.

If you think it is risky to innovate, think of the alternative. Today, the riskiest course of action is to *not* innovate. That is a direct route into the innovation gap, where irrelevancy, bankruptcy and oblivion await.

In his book *How to Run a Government So that Citizens Benefit and Taxpayers Don't Go Crazy* (2015)[20], Michael Barber points out that often, a bureaucracy's reaction to risk makes it *even more* vulnerable.

> "The instinctive reaction of a bureaucracy to a problem or a crisis is to become more cautious, more risk averse. Ironically, in an era

when change is as rapid as it has become in the early twenty-first century, this reaction ultimately adds to the risk of failure rather than reduces it." (P.191)

Clearly, we need a new way of thinking about risk. In a risk-averse culture such as in the public sector, leaders can still mitigate risk while innovating. They can:

1. Focus the innovation efforts and be strategic about what ideas are selected, groomed and implemented.

2. Use *evolutionary* rather than *revolutionary* innovation. In other words, move forward in iterative cycles of plan, act, observe and reflect, rather than taking a huge leap of faith into unchartered waters.

3. Run *pilots*, experiment, figure out what works and what doesn't, then scale up.

Christian Bason in *Leading Public Sector Innovation: Co-creating for a better society*[21] has some good advice about risk and failure for leaders who want to innovate. He says, "Fail early to succeed sooner." (p. 156) So figure out quickly (preferably through a pilot) what does or does not work and move on. Adapt and iterate, or abandon and cut losses.

Government departments live by what we refer to in my state as "The Courier Mail Test." *The Courier Mail* is Queensland's state-wide newspaper. If big things go horribly wrong in government, they end up on the front page of *The Courier Mail*. It has happened on several occasions. The possibility of that strikes fear into the hearts of ministers, senior public-sector leaders and pretty much everyone else in government with a strong sense of social responsibility.

I want to be very clear at this point that risk taking in the service of innovation is not an invitation for irresponsibility or lack of due diligence. Rather, it is about calculated risk taking and creating a "safe to fail" environment, applying the points above.

The irony is that over-engineering processes in an attempt to reduce failure and conserve resources can have the opposite effect. Conversely, it is the giving of permission to fail that can save time and resources, as the following case study demonstrates.

The ePulse group from Queensland Health used a fail-fast, agile approach to delivering its "virtual desktops" pilot. Virtual desktops enable people to access and operate information from any device or "thin terminals" (hardware with no software). It does away with the need to upgrade computers every few years. Historically, a project of that magnitude would have taken two years. But the project team delivered its outcome in three months at a fraction of the cost of implementing the traditional way. Team members were given permission to experiment with different ways of doing things. They figured out what worked and what didn't through trial and error, without the obligation to document proceedings at length (to ensure every "i" was dotted and "t" crossed), and implemented quickly. In this way, they were able to avoid developing a solution at enormous cost, which may not have been fit for purpose, and delivered a successful pilot. Virtual desktops are now in the process of being rolled out to other locations within Queensland Health.

The project leader's approach was try, fail, learn and showcase iteratively until the right outcome was reached. But even when something did fail, the failure was "repurposed" for benefit elsewhere. For example, any hardware or software licencing purchased for the project that proved ineffective was used elsewhere in the business. So, in this sense, "failure" is redefined. The experiment may not have served the purpose for which it was originally intended, but it served other purposes in unforeseen ways.

Identifying Opportunity

Much of my work in the past few years has been in the public sector. People sometimes have the view that entrepreneurialism can't flourish in government departments because of bureaucracy. While this may be true in some areas, there are many highly enterprising leaders within government departments at all levels who successfully innovate for the public good.

This was the story I came across recently when I was working in Singapore. It is a wonderful example of what an entrepreneurial person inside the public sector can achieve.

In 1960, Singapore's rapidly increasing population caused a housing crisis. Many thousands of people were living in over-crowded and sub-standard conditions. Lim Kim San, a civil at the time (who later went on to become a government minister), was appointed to the Housing and Development Board (HDB). He oversaw the mammoth task of constructing thousands of high-rise, low-cost apartments that eventually become the main source of housing for Singaporeans. The success of his undertaking came from his Minimum Viable Product (MVP) approach. MVP delivers a product with the basic features that will satisfy customers, thus reducing waste and getting the product to consumers as quickly as possible. Whatever is learnt about the process and product from the first iteration is incorporated into the next.

Lim did not allow himself to get bogged down in a detailed planning stage, which would tie up the project in red tape. Instead, he chose a "rough and ready" approach to work fast using rough estimates of the housing requirement. In this way, he built more units in the first year of the program than were built in the previous decade.

The interesting part of the story is that at the same time that Lim began his project, a committee was set up to find out whether the HDB had the capability and capacity to reach such a lofty construction goal. The committee took a year to publish its report that such a project could not be achieved in the timeframe. By that time, the entrepreneurial Lim had already completed the first 1000 units!

Human Helium

People in large bureaucratic organisations (be they government departments or large corporations) with an entrepreneurial mindset are like the helium in the balloon of progress.

They challenge the status quo and identify opportunities to add value. They question the norm, push the boundaries and take calculated risks. These are the people who create the future. They drive innovation.

There is a great TED Talk by Haley Van Dyck (Feb 2016) called "How a start-up in the White House is changing business as usual".[22] In it, she tells the story of how government processes are being deliberately disrupted from the inside out by the United States Digital Service. The approach the team is using is this:

1. Recruit the best and brightest talent from the US tech sector for short "tours of duty" inside government. They are drawn from Google, Twitter and Facebook – all bringing their combined knowledge, talent and experience to make government better (incidentally, more than half of them are women).

2. Pair the imported techie with a dedicated government employee who understands the system.

3. Place these dyads at strategic points within the public sector where the services are "mission critical and life changing" – where their impact can be maximised to transform outcomes for citizens.

4. Support them from every direction. These people get backing from the tech organisation they were sourced from – all the way to the President.

The experiment is paying off. The US Digital Service is already seeing great solutions to some of the US government's most wicked problems. One example is immigration, where a small team of six people worked closely with the agency to digitise its processes. The team started with people applying for replacement green cards – a process that used to take months. Within three months, the team had created a digital solution that was dramatically faster, cheaper and easier for the applicant.

How It Works

Entrepreneurialism within large organisations consists of three components.

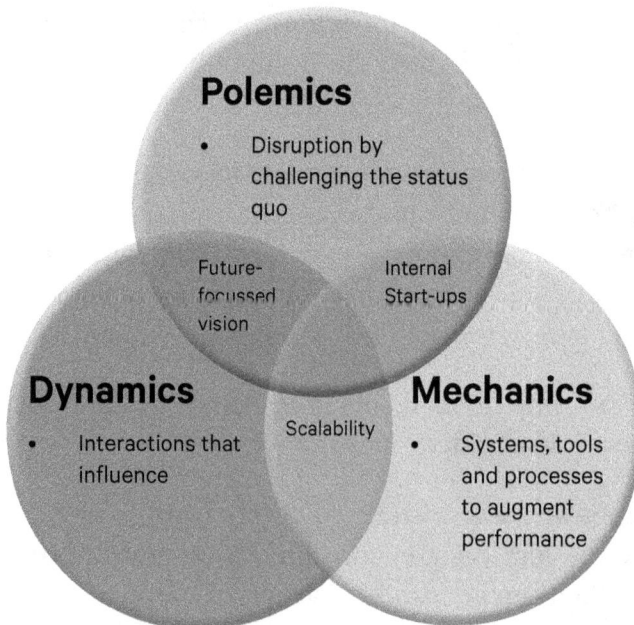

1. The impetus to change – *Polemics*. This is the challenge to the status quo that leads to disruption.

2. The steps to change – *Mechanics*. The systems, tools and processes that operationalise performance.

3. The diffusion of change – *Dynamics*. The interactions, conversations, communications and collaborations that influence others – stakeholders, citizens, other parts of the business or other agencies – to ensure that change gets traction.

At the intersection of these components are the outcomes and products of that pairing.

At the intersection of Polemics and Mechanics lies the concept of the *start-up*: a term not usually associated with government agencies or large corporations – but it can be.

This is where a small project driven by an entrepreneurial thinker interrogates the default and experiments with a completely different way of doing something. A start-up is simply a fledgling undertaking initiated by a small group of people, or a single person, working to solve a problem where the solution is not obvious and success is not guaranteed. It addresses a problem *worth* solving. But, if successful, there must be embedded in its DNA the ability to scale up and grow for major impact.

At the intersection of Mechanics and Dynamics lies *scalability*. This where a new way of doing something gets traction because it not only solves a pressing pain-point – it works out the fundamentals of how to do it. A new way of thinking and doing has emerged. As a result of the pilot (start-up), people now have a reasonable idea about what is required to forge a workable, longer-term solution. Also, the people involved in the project, or the people who support the undertaking, are able to influence others and advocate in a way that garners wide support. The emerging solution is adopted more widely with increasing impact, all the while gathering momentum.

At the intersection of Dynamics and Polemics lies the *future-focused vision*. This is where people can catch a glimpse of a better future, where it is possible to address difficult and complex problems in new and exciting ways. This vision emerges because it is articulated, influenced and shaped by visionary, disruptive, entrepreneurial thinkers.

The TED Talk case study in the previous section is a perfect example of this model in action.

In Australia, we are still at the tip of the iceberg when it comes to introducing new technology that will disrupt government services. Deloitte's 2015 report *Digital Government Transformation*[23], prepared for Adobe Systems Pty Ltd, gives us a sense of the opportunities in this area. To quote directly from the report on page 1:

> "Of the estimated 811 million transactions at the federal and state levels each year, approximately 40% are still completed using traditional channels. If this figure could be reduced to 20% over a 10-year period, productivity, efficiency and other benefits to government worth around $17.9 billion (in real terms) would be realised along with savings in time, convenience and out-of-pocket costs to citizens worth a further $8.7 billion – and all at a cost of $6.1 billion in new ICT and transitional arrangements. Taking benefits to governments and citizens together, the next stages of digital transformation deliver benefits worth around four times as much as they cost."

Unfortunately, we continue to under-utilise the capacity of technology to disrupt government services to deliver higher productivity and better services. This was a key message from the Australian Government's Productivity Commission report published in June 2016. The paper, *Digital Disruption: What do governments need to do?*[23], posits that Australia (along with many other Western governments) is not sufficiently utilising digital technologies to improve service delivery. On page 3, Productivity Commission chairman Peter Harris says:

> "By showing leadership in their own practices, re-designing regulation to enable rather than block the adoption of digital technologies, and mitigate community-level risks where practical, governments can do more than they appear to envisage today."

Entrepreneurial thinking and doing will help find and action innovation opportunities.

But it's not just about leveraging new technology. Entrepreneurialism comes in many different forms and different shapes and sizes.

Entrepreneurialism Beyond Technology

The previous examples are about the introduction of new technology, so it is only fair that I give an example of the model being operationalised in a non-technical context.

This example comes from the Department of Transport and Main Roads (TMR). A district director in regional Queensland noticed how much time and effort her team was spending on managing the resource-sharing processes in her region. The vastness of regional Queensland can pose unique challenges to operations. She saw an opportunity to "hack" the process – that's the cool way of saying disrupt it to make it quicker and easier (Polemics).

Her project, aptly entitled *Collaborative Resource Sharing*, introduced a new methodology for how people secured agreement for sharing resources. It was simple and elegant (Mechanics). She conducted the pilot with her area (Start-up). She "pitched" the idea and got the buy-in of the regional leadership team (Dynamics). She refined the process and rolled it out across a larger area (Scalability). And she is now looking for more opportunities to "hack" other processes to improve efficiency (Future-focused vision). Entrepreneurialism in action!

As part of the project reflection stage, I encouraged her to put the dollars around the benefit to the department. What was the commercial value? How much has this operational innovation saved TMR through increased productivity and efficiencies? These sorts of questions develop the business acumen of leaders.

Turns out, when implemented in her area alone, it yielded a saving of $15,000 a year. Over time, as it is adopted across other districts and with other functions across the state, the savings could amount to hundreds of thousands of dollars a year.

Strictly speaking, entrepreneurialism inside an organisation is referred to as *intrepreneurialism*, but it is not a well-known term. I had to add it to my spell check. However, we will hear it a lot more as the momentum gathers to nurture and encourage the skills that will breed innovation within organisations. I love working with the intrepreneurs who come through my innovation mentoring programs! To paraphrase poet Arthur O'Shaughnessy, "They are the dreamers of dreams, the movers and shakers of the world for ever, it seems."

Intrepreneurs are the thought leaders, the disrupters, the value creators, the human helium, the key people who will help shine a light on innovation opportunities inside organisations.

And they won't necessarily be part of the leadership team!

The Entrepreneurial Leader

What does it take to be an entrepreneurial leader? It takes passion, creativity and vision. It takes the demonstration of entrepreneurial behaviours to lead by example. It takes a preparedness to fail and learn and keep trying in the face of obstacles. It takes someone like Daniel Flynn, founder of Thankyou Water and 2014 Victorian Young Australian of the Year.

I met Flynn earlier this year at a conference where he told the inspirational story of how the social enterprise of Thankyou Water came to be and the difference it is making in the world. Sales from the bottles of water, which are now distributed through major supermarket chains, help fund clean water, hygiene and sanitation programs, body-care products and food-security programs in developing countries.

After seeing a video about the shortage of clean water in many countries, Flynn decided to be part of the solution. That was in 2007. Today, Thankyou has given more than 190,000 people access to clean water and 300,000 people access to hygiene and sanitation. It has also funded 19.1 million days' worth of food.

But the journey was anything but smooth and it was certainly never easy. A less determined person would have given up. Flynn and his small team had to raise funds, compete with big-name brands in a David-and-Goliath-type battle, pitch to sceptics, persist in the face of overwhelming resistance and create a movement. To get the buy-in of the two big Australian supermarket chains, Flynn used the power of social media and some audacious attention-getting strategies involving helicopters.

Nine years on, Flynn has made it possible for millions of people to also be a part of the solution.

His advice to 21st-century leaders and entrepreneurs (and intrepreneurs) is tailored and timely for our VUCA world.

Have a plan but be flexible. Be open to change and new ideas. Back yourself. Instead of fearing failure, adapt when things go wrong. Take responsibility for your vision (it's not up to someone else to make your idea work or believe in it). Constantly challenge your thinking: no idea is immediately perfect, so look for ways to refine it.[23]

We need entrepreneurial leaders who are bold and innovative to revitalise organisations. An entrepreneurial leader energises team members by providing them with an exciting, opportunity-focused vision.

Tips for Leaders

1. Think of entrepreneurialism as a new core skill for yourself and your team members.

2. Solve problems with an entrepreneurial mindset.

3. When something doesn't go according to plan, ask yourself and your team, "Where is the opportunity in this?"

4. Welcome calculated risk taking, "safe failure" and experiments in the form of pilots as the pathways to higher performance.

5. Use Polemics, Mechanics and Dynamics to drive entrepreneurialism (and intrepreneurialism).

In the Presence of Entrepreneurialism ...

Knowledge is valued. It provides the springboard to launch new initiatives.

Talent is harnessed. It is seen as a precious natural resource that will fire up innovation.

Experience is amplified. It grows as a result of new opportunities.

NOTES

NOTES

META-SKILL #2: DEMOCRATISATION

"You don't need a title to be a leader."

~ Public domain

CHAPTER 4

Meta-Skill #2 Democratisation

"When the effective leader is finished with his work,
the people say it happened naturally."

~ Lao Tzu

Today, anyone with an internet connection has access to vast stores of information. This democratisation of information has a flow-on effect to the democratisation of influence and decision making. Leaders need to become comfortable with democratised structures. This is a shift from the old command-and-control structure towards a more flexible and distributed model. Democratising leadership recognises that everyone on the team can play a leadership role, help make decisions, offer valuable contributions, advance the cause, proffer insights and drive outcomes. It is not only up to the designated leader to shoulder all responsibility for achieving the required results and making the decisions. People in general are intelligent and well-intentioned; they welcome and appreciate the opportunity to exercise their volition and offer their perspectives and input.

Rather than ideas trickling down from the top and losing momentum at each layer, in the innovation age there is the increasing realisation and expectation that great ideas can bubble up from anywhere in an organisation – provided there is a space for them to do so. And that is about creating a culture in which innovation can flourish. It is the difference between "leading from the top" versus "leading from the middle".

Leading from the Middle Versus Leading from the Top

Leading from the top is the equivalent of following a linear trajectory rather than an exponential one. Information flow is slow and one directional. It is a linear practice in an exponential world.

Leading from the middle is about *influencing* rather than directing those around you. It requires the leader to lead by example. It is the creation of an environment where innovation and people flourish. It challenges traditional notions of what it means to be a leader. It requires the leader to become an expert at getting buy-in for ideas without being coercive. In his book *Work with Me*, Simon Dowling[26] offers some wonderful advice to leaders on the gentle art of creating buy-in.

> "Buy-in requires patience, empathy and careful thinking. You need to know when to yield control in order to maintain it. You need a healthy dose of emotional intelligence. You need to be willing to go slow to go fast."

That is not to say that hierarchical organisations such as large corporations or government agencies are doomed to be trapped in an outdated command-and-control structure. It is entirely possible for the two structures to coexist. They are not mutually exclusive. However, for that to happen, it does require a paradigm shift in the thinking of the organisation's leaders. They need to be prepared to relinquish "control" and share the leadership responsibilities with team members. It also means being prepared to be a follower, as well as a leader. This works when there are open pathways of communication, ease of a two-way, open exchange of knowledge, wisdom and ideas, and when there is trust among team members and the leader.

In his book *Designing the Networked Organization*[27], Ken Everett refers to this process of open communication as "hosting" – where the leader consciously builds community by initiating and hosting conversations rather than decreeing what is to be. Think of it as the difference between the Sherpa who gently guides the team on the journey, keeping them safe in dangerous territory, versus the general who leads the charge into battle. It is where the leader operates at the "edge of chaos": "Neither out of control nor completely in control. The edge of chaos is where learning and innovation can happen."

Facilitating high-quality conversations is fundamental to leading from the middle. Great conversation starters include: "Let's talk about your work. What part of your work gives you energy? What part takes it away? What can we do about it?"

There are many benefits of this approach, including a better flow of information through the workplace.

Opening the Channels of Communication

Hosting high-quality conversations facilitates open communication and proactive information sharing. This leads to better outcomes for stakeholders, better use of resources and better relationships. Good communication builds a robust organisation because people will make better decisions, network effectively and solve problems early before issues become critical.

It is true that some people hoard information under the mistaken belief that the person with the information is the person with the power. But generally speaking, today there is a recognition that in our complex workplaces, information sharing and open communication facilitate higher productivity. In fact, it is the person who *shares* the most information who is often the person with the most influence.

The recognition of the value of information sharing harks to the birth of the democratic state in ancient Athens – the first known democracy in the world. The Greek ideal in the city state was for the entire citizenry to act as the collective medium of information dissemination by debating issues in public, as well as exchanging, interpreting and discussing the news of the day. The cornerstone of this societal structure was the noble idea that the entire system would benefit and prosper if each person had access to the truth and could act on it.

Fast forward 25 centuries and we see good communication on the list of essential workplace skills. And there is good reason for this.

In 2013, the Project Management Institute released a report called *The High Cost of Low Performance: The Essential Role of Communications.*[28] The report states that one of the highest risk factors in huge projects worth billions of dollars is a lack of effective communication. So of all the risks projects face, a massive 56% comes down to poor communication. Despite this insight, many organisations admit they are "not placing adequate importance on effectively communicating critical project information".

Think about your team meetings.

- Are they opportunities for everyone to participate and offer a perspective?

- Is there a balance of asking for information as well as disseminating it?

- Are conflicting viewpoints regarded as opportunities for robust exploration of issues rather than sources of conflict?

- Do people *actively* listen to others?

- Is feedback seen as an opportunity for development rather than criticism?

- Are introverts encouraged to speak and participate?

- Are the new recruits, who come with fresh eyes, asked for their observations about what could be done differently or better?

Relinquishing "Control"

Relinquishing control is not about promoting chaos. It is about knowing the capabilities of your people and inviting participation. It's about creating the conditions and context for people to feel empowered to step up to challenges. Some leaders are uncomfortable with this because they feel it is an abdication of their responsibilities, while others feel it does not bring enough personal glory.

Jim Collins, author of best seller *Good to Great*[29], identifies the highest form of leadership as Level Five Leadership. This is where leaders are not driven by ego (which is Level Four Leadership), but by a blend of personal humility and professional will. They are ambitious first and foremost for the cause, ie. the *work* that they do, not for *themselves*. Level Five leaders know when to relinquish control. They are skilled at passing the ball to team members so they can feel a sense of ownership of the work being done, as well as the outcomes. However, they are equally skilled at knowing how and when to extend a steadying, experienced hand to ensure projects remain on track.

As we move further into the innovation age, this new style of leadership will become increasingly important. Organisations will strive to become employers of choice so they can attract talented people. Leaders of the future will be comfortable inviting deeper involvement and participation in decision making, seeing it as a powerful people-development tool rather an abdication of a leader's responsibility.

One senior leader who was a chief superintendent in the Queensland Fire and Emergency Services said to me recently that he now saw his role as that of a "bulldozer" – clearing the path ahead of obstacles so his team members could implement their great ideas. In his words, "I am slowly becoming one of the 'dinosaurs' because of my length of service, but I recognise there are young, talented and dynamic staff working for me who better understand new technology and have some great ideas about how to improve our service delivery. So I now assist and guide them to get their ideas and innovations implemented."

I think the best description of what he does is "scrum master". That's the new term (borrowed from American football) for the person whose job it is to eliminate stumbling blocks, impediments and barriers, keep projects on track and maintain momentum and focus. The leader who does this serves as a facilitator rather than a decision maker, a catalyst rather than a controller, a mentor rather than a micromanager.

Why Democratisation does not Appeal to all Leaders

A democratised style of leadership does not appeal to leaders who need validation, approbation and recognition. It does not appeal to those who are afraid others will get the credit, or for whom it is imperative to be seen as smart, talented and infallible.

Some leaders may be afraid that if they don't have all the answers, or if others *think* they don't have all the answers, they may be perceived as a weak leader. This is especially the case if a leader has risen through the ranks by being the "fixer" or built their career and reputation on being the "go-to" person.

There can be a self-gratifying buzz to solving someone else's problem. Besides, it is often easier and quicker to provide an answer than to formulate a good question to serve as a learning experience. If a team member comes to you and says, "Hey boss, we're behind schedule on this project. What should we do?", it may be much more time effective in the short term to tell the team member what to do rather than help them to work it out by guiding them through the problem-solving process. But chances are that next time there's a scheduling problem, team members will have to come to you again because they haven't learnt how to be autonomous. So ultimately, in the long-term, it is not a time effective strategy at all.

Do You See What I See?

Usually before I begin a culture-change project within an organisation, I start with a survey to identify practices and perceptions. It also provides good baseline data so we can chart the journey, and it helps identify innovation opportunities. I separate data gathered from the leaders and data gathered from staff to identify differences in perception.

The area that consistently yields the greatest amount of difference is participation. In a nutshell, leaders usually think they invite participation, contribution and collaboration more than what is perceived by the employees. Staff believe they are consulted less than what is thought by the leaders. The greatest discrepancy is usually yielded by the statement, "Employee input is sought when addressing challenges or during the implementation of innovation." The perception among leaders is that they do this well; the perception among employees is that they don't.

Similarly, the 2016 Hudson Report[30] showed that while 70% of employers thought they had a culture where new ideas were openly shared and discussed, only 47% of employees agreed.

The power of democratisation, collaborative decision-making and enfranchisement of workers is not a new concept. Back in the first century, the Roman agriculturalist Columella reputedly consulted his slaves because, from his observation, "they were more willing to set about a piece of work on which they think their opinions have been asked and their advice followed."[31] It is human nature to value what you help create. People want to be involved and consulted.

Recently, a clinical division of a branch within a large government agency underwent an external review. A number of recommendations came from this review, one being that the division needed to develop a Vision, Mission and Purpose statement (VMP). Rather than senior management or a committee producing the statement, input was sought from the *entire* division via a number of channels. More than 50% of people responded to the call for involvement – which is high. People were kept informed of the initiative's progress with ongoing opportunity to shape the developing VMP. The result was a VMP statement people felt they could genuinely own; one that reflected their collective voice.

'Humanity at Work'

One organisation that has taken democratisation to a whole new level is award-winning Mondragon Corporation[32], based in Spain but with a global presence in the industrial, finance and retail sectors. The company's values of participation, innovation and social responsibility are summed up in its slogan, "humanity at work". It is, in essence, a co-operative where the employees own and directly benefit from the success of the corporation.

Mondragon's innovative business model sees the employees elect the senior leaders. Executive pay is limited to a ratio of about 5:1 (in Australia, executive pay is about 30 times the average worker's salary), and all staff can have a say on major issues that affect the company. Not only has this egalitarian business model produced engaged employees who enjoy greater job security and have a genuine interest in the organisation's success, it has also led to remarkable increases in productivity and international competitiveness.

As the movement to humanise workplaces gathers momentum, it's likely we will see the rise of the employee-owned corporation – a kinder, gentler, more democratised workplace. Workers in employee-owned companies are more engaged, more productive and more innovative – and this makes them more profitable.

In Scotland, the number of these kinds of firms has doubled in the past six years. In the US, they are growing about 6% a year and account for about 12% of the private workforce. Research seems to show fairly conclusively that the combination of ownership and participative management results in substantial gains.[33]

Democratising the workplace does not necessarily mean turning an organisation into an employee-owned company. It can be achieved by involving people in decision making, hosting conversations to open the channels of communication, consulting with people and encouraging collaboration.

Tips for Leaders

1. Lead through influence rather than control.

2. Give others the opportunity to solve problems. Guide and mentor as needed.

3. People support what they help create, so involve others in decision making.

4. Delegate innovation initiatives.

5. Build trust and a sense of community by "hosting" conversations.

In the Presence of Democratisation ...

Knowledge is volunteered. If people have autonomy, they are more likely to offer solutions.

Talent is nurtured. Natural ability is given the chance to be demonstrated and appreciated.

Experience is deepened. It is extended as a result of the opportunity to participate.

NOTES

_____

_____

_____

_____

_____

_____

_____

_____

_____

_____

_____

_____

_____

_____

_____

META-SKILL #3
UTILISATION

"A leader's role is to raise people's aspirations for what they can become and to release their energies so they will try to get there."

~ David R. Gergen

CHAPTER 5

Meta-Skill #3 Utilisation

"Talented performers flock to the best and brightest
leaders, and these leaders in turn lift the lids off their
people and uncork the latent talent inside of them."

~ John Maxwell

I recently had a corporate client meeting in a very up-market and modern building. We had our meeting not in a claustrophobic little meeting room but in the large, well-appointed kitchen and lunch area, which afforded magnificent, sweeping views over the city. My host made a cup of tea for me and a coffee for himself. It was prepared from scratch – not instant. We chatted as he ground the beans, loaded and tamped the aromatic powder into the espresso machine. We continued talking with slightly raised voices over the noise of the pressurised water extracting the flavour from the grounds. I was secretly impressed by his mastery of the barista arts.

When he finished, I watched where he would dispose of the grounds so that I could toss my spent tea bag into the bin along with them. "Oh no, we don't throw them away. We recycle them into the worm farm," he explained. With that, he pulled open a cleverly disguised drawer that housed the corporate worm farm and dispensed of our left-overs. Apparently, worms thrive on coffee grounds, tea bags, fruit peelings, vegetable scraps and all sorts of other unexpected residues (even vacuum-cleaner dust) that would normally be discarded into rubbish bins.

Imagine all the coffee grounds and tea bags around the world that could be put to better use than taking up space in bins and rubbish dumps? Especially given that coffee is one of the most-traded products in the world. And yes, I know that many forward-thinking manufacturers, producers and organisations are finding innovative solutions for waste – but we have a long way to go.

But more importantly, what we need are innovative solutions for the ridiculous waste of talent that occurs in most organisations. There is a vast amount of un-utilised or under-utilised knowledge, experience and wisdom languishing in every workplace. How can these valuable resources be utilised? How can latent capabilities be activated and deployed for the benefit of everyone – individuals, teams and the organisation?

A Worthy Investment

The term "utilisation" sounds rather exploitative. But the sense in which I am using it is not about taking advantage of people, but tapping into the skills, knowledge and experience that resides in team members across the organisation. Employees have a deep understanding and first-hand knowledge of the processes, procedures and tasks associated with their specific roles. These are the people who know what prompts complaints from customers, causes the bottlenecks and blocks crucial information. If the organisation wants to innovate internal work processes and service delivery, then these employees are the source of such innovation.

Bill Gates said that Microsoft's primary assets were the software development skills of the employees. But these assets don't show up on the balance sheet. An organisation's real value is the combined reservoir of the knowledge, talent and experience that resides within it. The wise leader of the innovation age finds ways to nurture and harvest these precious natural resources.

Every year, I work with a small cohort of 3M's Asia-Pacific leaders as they prepare to report to the senior leadership team on the innovations they have developed during their time in one of 3M's leadership development programs. It is part of 3M's process for developing a pipeline of internal leadership talent. Developing talent has a high priority within the company – *at all levels*. The CEO, Inge Thulin, spends about one-fifth of his time on talent development – personally teaching in some of the leadership programs. It is an investment worth making.

Elicit Greatness

I have seen talented leaders come into failing projects that are running over budget and behind schedule and turn the whole situation around. The key is simple: get to know people, understand their talents, strengths and interests, then restructure the division of labour and allocation of tasks accordingly.

Sure, it takes time and a preparedness to host one-on-one conversations. But when you consider that the alternative is a failed project, it is time well spent. Good leaders open up the channels of communication so that they *know* what they are working with. It becomes easier to lead when you know the talent you have in your team. Scottish novelist John Buchan, who served as Governor General of Canada, puts it thus: "The task of leadership is not to put greatness into people, but to elicit it, for the greatness is there already." When we find ways to do that, people are more engaged and passionate, and will often increase their discretionary spend of effort simply because they enjoy what they are doing.

So how do you, as a leader, acquire these valuable insights into getting the most out of your people? You ask them.

The Knowledge Bank

A simple way to uncover the valuable resources in your team is to create a knowledge bank. Ask people to volunteer information about themselves. No pressure. You can collect this information via an online tool such as Survey Monkey or a hard-copy page.

Ask questions like:

- What travel experience have you had? Have you lived in other cultures?

- What non-related work skills do you have?

- Have you worked in other industries? Who were your previous clients?

- Do you have other formal qualifications that are not related to your current work role?

- What are some interesting things about you that your work colleagues don't know?

- What are your hobbies?

- Do you have some areas of special interest?

When I do this with groups, I make sure the survey doesn't look like a standard information-gathering survey with the questions laid out in a boring list form. We use a graphically designed template that is visually engaging. Make the exercise fun!

So many interesting outcomes and stories have come from this simple exercise. Here are a few.

The deputy director of one organisation I worked with, upon completing this exercise, said she was amazed at the qualifications held by some of the junior admin staff. These employees were considered to be in "non-professional" roles, yet had qualifications and specialist skills the organisation had no idea about. Perhaps such things were discussed at the job interview but were long since forgotten.

For example, one of the junior staff had completed a graphic design course and had a strong creative flair, which was not being used in her official role as a PA. When the staff were invited to find ways of using their skills, she took it upon herself to create a series of beautifully designed posters to communicate the company's new vision and mission to display around the building. And she didn't ask for permission to do it. She just did it. Voluntarily. And enjoyed it. And so did everyone else.

Another SME (small to medium-sized enterprise) discovered that it had a number of avid gardeners on staff. So the new CEO funded the repurposing of a portion of the car park into a vegetable garden. The project grew beyond all expectations and gathered in the "non-gardeners". People started to spend break times gardening – sharing information about gardening and work issues.

The activity became a great stress reliever. The plot eventually became so productive that employees were able to gather fresh vegetables to take home. Productivity, morale and collegiality skyrocketed.

In one government department, a team leader said to me she had discovered that one of her team members lived her life according to a philosophy called "voluntary simplicity". This is where someone chooses to live their life in as simply as possible, eschewing the materialism and consumerism of modern society. The leader went on to tell me that when she found that out, she invited that person onto a project tasked with streamlining and simplifying their department's processes and procedures. Her rationale was that someone who lived their life by the principles of simplicity would likely identify the unnecessary clutter of bloated organisational processes.

Simple initiatives such as this can open up the channels of communication and have a *huge* payoff.

"Uberise" Your Team

The word "uber" doesn't only refer to the alternative to taxis. The term is synonymous with tapping into unused capacity. Undoubtedly, there is unused capacity in your team. Creating some form of a knowledge bank will help you find it and tap into it.

In a workshop last year, a participant told me the story of how one of the training rooms in his workplace was unusable for weeks because of an electrical fault. Turns out, in his previous career he had been an electrician and he still maintained his licence, doing odd jobs on weekends. He could have fixed the problem in about half an hour. He only found out about the situation after the event, otherwise he would have volunteered.

Are there skills in your team that aren't being utilised? Graphic design, public speaking, teaching, negotiation, photography, film-making, research, painting, networking, cooking and business are skills that people may bring from a previous career or hobby. It may not be immediately apparent how you might use them, but one thing is for certain: if you don't know about them, you certainly won't.

The CEO of one SME I worked with said to me jokingly, "The only thing we could do is form a band." He had discovered that 75% of his employees played musical instruments. Guess what they did for their Christmas function? What impact would that have had on team cohesion?

In the future, we will see the uberisation of the workplace in different ways. Fully using the skills of your team members is one way. It may also take the form of "agile insourcing" – bringing in one or several team members from another part of the organisation to help with a particular aspect of a project. Organisations need an organisational architecture that is flexible enough to enable this to happen.

Seriously, What Planet Are You From?

If people are not accustomed to working in a democratised environment where their input is invited, valued and utilized, it can take some getting used to. That kind of culture change doesn't happen overnight. One general manager of a fast-growing SME I worked with described her experience of implementing some of these principles.

She said that as part of the process of making innovation *everyone's* responsibility, not just the CEO's, she started asking people for input into how things could be improved throughout the business. She asked them to bring forth their ideas. Her exact words were, "They looked at me like I was from Mars!"

To her credit, she didn't give up and started hosting one-on-one conversations. Although initially people wouldn't offer ideas in meetings, she found that if she spoke with them individually they had lots of input. Over a relatively short time of six weeks, she was able to open the communication channels within the business to bring a number of benefits.

Once people got used to the idea of sharing information and offering ideas one-on-one, they became more comfortable doing it in meetings. The process also made it possible for her to start divesting herself of operational considerations so she could free up her time to be more strategic. "We are growing so quickly I have to see the big picture," she said. In their regular team meetings, they also started communicating the firm's vision and goals so that everyone was on the same page. This was a business that learnt to utilise the talent of its people. The year after this happened, it had a 50% increase in growth.

Another general manager I worked with from a steel fabrication firm said to me:

"We are now gathering information about how to improve our business from our workers on the shop floor so we are driving innovation from both the top and the bottom. We are much better at tapping into our employees' knowledge and experience. They feel like they have something to come to work *for*, other than just welding a bit of the steel. Before they used to go through the motions, but now you see them being proactive rather than reactive."

This is the power of utilisation! People feel as though they are bringing their *whole* selves to work. It is empowering and a huge productivity booster.

Carrots are for Bunnies and Sticks for Dogs to Fetch

Think of a time when you were engaged in an activity for the sheer love of it.

No one had to force you, manipulate you or coerce you into doing it. It was a joy, a pleasure, even if it was, at times, difficult and exhausting, requiring great amounts of concentration and commitment – whether you were committed to climbing Mount Everest, preparing to perform in an amateur theatre production, training for a sporting event, growing your own vegetables, researching your favourite subject or even writing a book.

Participation in the activity itself brought its own rewards. When we are motivated to take action because of the sense of fulfilment, satisfaction and efficacy it brings, we are *intrinsically motivated.*

The opposite of this is *extrinsic motivation,* where we engage in an activity for the promise of a reward or fear of punishment. It is a classic carrot-and-stick approach to changing behaviour. In education-speak, it is called "conditioning" (not the kind that makes your hair shiny).

When it comes to motivating employees in the workplace, there is a place for both kinds of motivation – intrinsic and extrinsic. Indeed, they go hand in hand. We can use extrinsic motivators such as praise and recognition to help people develop a positive view of themselves and their achievements so that they then experience intrinsic rewards from their labours.

As a leader, who would you rather deal with and work with on a daily basis: the person who comes to work to pick up a pay cheque, or the person who comes to work because they see value in what they do and derive a sense of purpose from it?

When it comes to leading in the innovation age, a useful skill is knowing how to transition people from being extrinsically motivated to being intrinsically motivated.

A general approach is outlined below in the Levels of Cognisance model. My caveat is this: as with all models, it isn't a panacea and the process won't work all the time, but that doesn't mean it isn't a useful framework.

The term "cognisance" refers to perception, awareness and knowledge. Thus, levels of cognisance refer to the different stages people transition through to become increasingly intrinsically motivated, culminating in a self-concept where they identify themselves as innovators. People who do that are motivated to effect positive change because that is "who they are" – they can't help themselves.

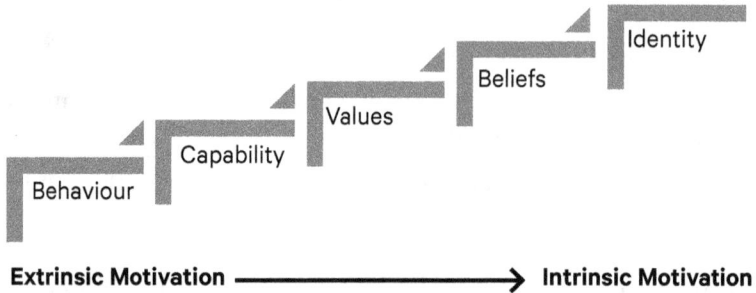

Extrinsic Motivation ──────────────→ **Intrinsic Motivation**

Let's think about this transition in the context of motivating people to be involved with innovation in the workplace.

The table on the following page identifies a series of transitioning motivators that help people to grow their confidence and self-efficacy in relation to implementing innovation. Transitioning motivators are the actions you as leader can take to facilitate their development to the next level.

Level	Definition	Transitioning Motivators	Motivation Driver
Indentity	Becomes a part of one's character and one's unique self.		Intrinsic Motivation
		Acknowledgement and Articulation	
Beliefs	Becomes a fundamental principle to live by.		
		Reward and Recognition	
Values	Considered to be an important personal quality.		
		Responsiblity	
Capability	Has become a competenency.		
		Practice/Training	
Behaviour	Enacting or doing at a basic level. G oing through the motions.		Extrinsic Motviation

Table 1: Levels of Cognisance

At the bottom of the table, on the lowest rung is *Behaviour*. This is where people go through the motions with limited engagement in a particular activity. For example, they may be present in brainstorming meetings but don't contribute much. It may be that they don't have the skill or the confidence to participate more fully and offer their ideas.

The first thing to do is provide them with some skill development. This could be in the form of formal *training* (going to a course or workshop) or informal mentoring followed by the opportunity to *practice* their developing skills with support as needed to develop their confidence. You could encourage them to co-facilitate (with you or another experienced team member) an idea-generation session or even an ordinary team meeting, mentoring them through the process and giving feedback.

Once someone practices a skill sufficiently, they become *competent* at it. It then becomes a *capability*. How long this takes will vary from person to person. It depends on their readiness and receptivity for the activity, their previous experiences and their belief in their ability to learn.

To transition someone to the next level from *capability*, give them some *responsibility*. Show your confidence in their abilities. Demonstrate that you trust them to get the job done by allowing them to proceed without micromanaging them. You are there as a safety net, not as an examiner. If they have already "cut their teeth" co-facillitating a brainstorming session, then it is time for them to lead the next think tank. This includes doing the prep: getting people ready for the meeting, arranging any equipment that might be needed, clarifying the issues under consideration, establishing guidelings, taking the lead during the session and following through after the event.

As people grow into their *responsibility* and demonstrate their developing capacity, they will see this new aptitude or area of expertise as a beneficial addition to their skill set. It may begin to inform their professional practice in other ways as they look for opportunities to transfer their skills. They may volunteer to conduct other related activities. At this point, doing a good job at this activity and related activities becomes a *value* – a source of personal or professional pride.

Then, when people around them such as colleagues, team leaders, supervisors and peers give positive feedback, praise and *recognition* – their *belief* in themselves grows. Having learnt the process, they may offer to mentor others through a similar journey. At this point, the ability to run brainstorming meetings and other activities that encourage innovation is enjoyable and rewarding. Participation has become the new normal and a fundamental principle to live by.

The final step is to lock in the new self-concept so that it is integral to a person's *identity*. It is now who they are. The person thinks of themselves as an innovator to the extent that they would find ways of innovating even if they worked in an environment that didn't support it. They would "fly under the radar" because they can't help themselves. To facilitate this transition, use *acknowledgement* and *articulation*. Speak about the person in ways that establish them as an innovator. The following story illustrates this.

Recently, I held a public workshop caled *Leading for Innovation.* People from many different industries attended – corporate, public sector, education. One of the participants was a school principal. He had brought along with him a young teacher. When it came time for people to introduce themselves to the group, the principal took it upon himself to introduce his young staff member. This is what he said: "I've brought Bruce along with me today because although he has only been teaching for four years and has been with our school for just two of those, he had already established himself as a leader within our school community. He has transformed our Arts department and raised the reputation of our school in the eyes of the community. I want to ensure that he has the opportunity to develop his skills as an innovator because there is no doubt in my mind that Bruce is going to make a huge contribution in highly innovative ways to education and the lives of students over the coming years."

I watched Bruce as the principal spoke about him, articulated his contributions, acknowledged his talents, spoke of his faith in him and voiced his well-founded expectations for his future. Bruce was literally glowing! I believe that what the principal was deliberately and consciously doing was using the transitioning motivators of *articulation* and *acknowledgement*. He was a very smart a man doing a very smart thing. He was ensuring his protégé was locking in an identity as an innovative leader, intrinsically motivated to enact transformative change.

Here is an end-to-end case study of this model in action.

Yvonne is a nursing educator who runs a leadership program with clinical nurses. The nurses have to complete a project within the 12-month timeframe of the program. One of the nurses in the program, Chris, had responsibility for oncology families around the state. She wanted to create an app to share and gather information quickly. But she thought it would be completely out of her capacity to do anything like that. It was too big a job. She didn't have the technological skills or the project management skills. There would be too many people to influence and bring on board. She would be too far out of her depth. Her thinking was, "This may be a great idea – but it is just too big and I don't even know where to start."

Yvonne started by giving Chris some basic training in how to tackle projects. She mentored her through the process of breaking down the various phases and components of the assignment into achievable tasks. The initially overwhelming prospect started to look much more doable. Chris started to gain confidence in her ability to progress her idea. She realised that she didn't have to know how to build the app herself – she just needed to know who to talk to and who to connect and collaborate with.

Chris slowly developed her capabilities in project management and her confidence in her ability to deliver an outcome. She had full responsibility for the success of the undertaking. Yvonne would meet with her regularly to talk through her progress: what the barriers were, what was and wasn't going well, and what she was learning along the way. Chris could chart her development and appreciated the value of her own growth, as well as the value of the project. Not only was this endeavour going to make life easier for stressed families, it was providing her with the vehicle for her own development.

When Chris implemented the app with the oncology families she was working with, they gave her extremely positive feedback. The app had made such a tremendous difference in their lives. It enabled them to directly input results from various tests, easily contact relevant specialists at the nearest hospitals if they were away on holidays, capture their health history and record doctors' visits – all conveniently located in the one place for quick reference.

The rewards were extrinsic and intrinsic. The families were very grateful, publically recognising her efforts. At the same time, Chris received a great sense of personal fulfilment in being able to make a positive difference to their lives. By this stage, Chris had a fundamental belief in herself as an innovater.

The step that ultimately cemented her identity came from the acknowledgement Chris received from the broader health community across the country, as well as internationally. Her innovative app won a number of awards. She received invitations to present at conferences nationally and internationally, and organisations around the world are requesting the app. People now come to her for guidance and she mentors others.

The app is in phase two of development and Chris is looking for ways to make it even more effective and comprehensive. She is no longer frightened of seemingly impossible projects, of asking questions, of seeking sources of funding, submitting grant applications, garnering support and looking for alternative pathways in the face of barriers. She has changed the lives of her patients and their families, and changed the lives of her team members in the process.

It is an excellent example of a talented leader unleashing, developing and leveraging the talent within an organisation.

Tips for Leaders

1. Take the time to get to know team members and find out what lights them up.

2. Encourage team members to get to know each other so that they have a sense of the knowledge, talent and experience that surrounds them.

3. Open the channels of communication to discover the extent of the capabilities present in your workplace or your team.

4. Use team meetings as opportunities for information sharing in both directions.

5. Facilitate higher levels of intrinsic motivation in team members by using the transitioning motivators in the Levels of Cognisance model.

In the Presence of Utilisation ...

Knowledge is activated. Tacit knowledge, the kind of knowledge that can't be captured in procedure manuals, becomes available.

Talent flourishes. When people can work on projects that excite or appeal to them, they bring much more effort, commitment and passion to the table.

Experience is tapped into. It is recruited and developed through interest and opportunity.

NOTES

META-SKILL #4
CREATIVITY

"Access to talented and creative people is to modern workplaces
what access to coal and iron ore was to steel-making."
~ Richard Florida [34]

CHAPTER 6

Meta-Skill #4 Creativity

"The role of a creative leader is not to have all the ideas; it's to create a culture where everyone can have ideas and feel that they're valued."

~ Sir Ken Robinson

In 2010, IBM concluded an extensive global survey of more than 1,500 chief executive officers from 60 countries. It took two years of data gathering from CEOs in different sectors and industries around the world. The intention was to better understand the challenges, goals and thinking of CEOs. The subsequent report was called *Capitalizing on Complexity: Insights from the Global Chief Executive Officer Study.*[35] One clear finding was the chief executives believed it was creativity – more than rigour, management discipline, integrity or even vision – that was needed to successfully navigate an increasingly complex world. Indeed, creative thinking had become a core leadership competency!

The report was widely referred to and referenced. It was a harbinger, heralding the arrival of creativity in the boardroom. In 2010, creativity became mainstream! The innovation age had arrived.

Traditionally, people have been rewarded above all for analytical and logical thinking. And, of course, these capacities are still important, but today there is recognition that these qualities are simply *not enough* to solve complex problems in a rapidly changing world. They must be integrated with and augmented by creative thinking. This characterises the shift from the information age to the innovation age.

The complex challenges facing contemporary workplaces need creative thinking, not just logical and analytical thinking. We need leaders who are mentally agile enough to know when to *switch* among the different modalities. The innovation age needs leaders who are comfortable with non-linear thinking and ambiguity, who are prepared to cross boundaries to solve problems that require holistic thinking, who can adapt methods in order to accommodate unforeseen consequences, and who are flexible in their approaches.

In the book *The Innovator's DNA: Mastering the Five Skills of Disruptive Innovators*[36], Dyer, Gregersen and Christensen make it very clear that creativity is an essential 21st-century leadership trait. "Bottom Line: if you want innovation, you need creativity skills within the top management team of your company." (P.7) Sadly, for some organisations DNA seems to stand for Does Not Apply.

The past couple of decades have produced an abundance of good research in respected publications that have paved the way for creativity to emerge as the new essential skill for the innovation age.

In 1995, an article in the *Journal of Creative Behavior* reported that employee creativity and corporate innovation emerged as prime factors in accomplishing organisational goals.[37] In 1999, The *Creativity Research Journal* reported a study that showed creative thinking skills were twice as predictive of success than IQ scores.[38] A less scholarly article appeared in *The Economist* in 2006, maintaining that the biggest challenge in organisations is to develop individuals with the brain power and especially the ability to think creatively.[39] The *Journal of Strategic Leadership* in 2008[40] reported that the stock price of companies perceived to have creative leadership on average grew 900% over a 10-year period, compared with just 74% growth in companies perceived to lack creative leadership.

In 2011, the Society for Knowledge Economics in Australia produced a document called *Leadership, Culture and Management Practices of High Performing Workplaces in Australia: Indicative Guidelines through Case Studies of High and Mid Performing Workplaces.*[41] Its research showed that high-performing workplaces have cultures and leadership styles that support the innovation ambitions and *creativity* among staff. The 2016 World Economic Forum report *The Future of Jobs: Employment, Skills and Workforce Strategy for the Fourth Industrial Revolution*[42] states that by 2020, creativity will be third on the list of top ten skills, behind complex problem solving and critical thinking.

Gone are the days when people believed you left your creativity behind when you went to work. It is now widely acknowledged that creative people and creative teams are more engaged and more productive, delivering better outcomes. Creative thinking is the new black.

Are You Creative?

One of the questions I often ask people in my workshops is, "Who is happy to acknowledge publicly that they are creative?" Most times, few hands go up. Most people don't think they are creative. This is a fallacy. *Everyone can be creative!* If you ask seven year olds if they are creative – most will say yes. If you ask adults – most will say no. What happens? People lose their belief in their creative abilities.[43] The irony is that people who don't think of themselves as creative are often highly creative but do not give themselves credit for it.

A wonderful example of this is my friend Uko from Nigeria. I first met Uko when I was in Hyderabad in India to deliver the opening keynote at a conference. I was also scheduled to deliver a breakout session on creative thinking in the afternoon. At lunchtime, Uko bounded up to me to say he had registered for my afternoon workshop and was very much looking forward to it. He said he needed to hear what I had to say because he was "not creative" (his words) and wanted to learn how to become so.

We spent some time in conversation. I asked him what he did. Uko was a community aid worker in regional Nigeria. His job was to work with villages to help them become more self-sufficient and source potential funding from global aid agencies. But whenever he called a community meeting to discuss important issues that affected the villagers or to disseminate information, they wouldn't come. So he came up with a simple but ingenious solution.

He stopped calling community meetings. Instead, he started putting on soccer matches. Surprise, surprise ... everyone turned up. At half time, he would say, "Well, seeing as you are all here anyway, let's discuss these important issues that affect all of you before we finish the game."

In this way, he increased community engagement in the strategic decision-making processes in his region and was able to share important information on how to tap into global community aid and support. What's more, he made the process enjoyable.

It was a simple, elegant and extremely effective solution that didn't cost any additional money, time or effort, but delivered tangible outcomes. All this from a man who said that he "wasn't creative".

I share that story because it illustrates so well that many leaders solve problems creatively everyday but do not recognise or give themselves credit for their creativity. Every time you solve an unfamiliar problem, or look at a situation through someone else's eyes to get a fresh perspective, or experiment with a different way of doing something to get a better outcome, you are being creative. Unfortunately, people often think that only major artistic undertakings count as real creativity. They think creativity is only for artists, writers and musicians.

News flash. Not so. We can all be creative!

Let's expand our definition of creativity. We need to move from the notion that creativity is the exclusive domain of the lone genius working on the next technological breakthrough in their parents' garage. Or a prodigy like Mozart, who is able to perfectly capture the music he heard in his head without having to do any revisions. It makes a good story, but it's not true. Mozart worked very hard at his compositions. He spent at least five hours every morning composing music and spent months or years refining many of the pieces he is best known for.

"Big C" versus "Little c" Creativity

There is a difference between everyday creativity, which we will call "little c" versus paradigm-shifting creativity that wins you a Nobel prize, which we will call "big C" creativity.

Everyday creativity can be as simple as bringing a fresh perspective to problems we encounter on a day-to-day basis. While it may not secure us the Nobel prize, it could make us more productive in the workplace.

When my daughter was six years old, I gave her a set of long balloons to make balloon animals. We've all seen those bulbous, alien-looking creatures sculpted from the twists and turns of inflated rubber. We were going to have fun making these creatures. The phone rang and I left her for a little while (this was back in the days when we still used land lines).

When I returned, I was greeted with an unexpected sight. Not a single balloon animal. Instead, a musical instrument! She had tied the long balloons across the arms of a chair to create a makeshift harp. And because the arms were slightly splayed, the "strings" had varying tensions, enough to produce different pitches as she plucked them. My first reaction was, "That's not what you're *supposed* to do with them." Then I realised what she had done was even more creative. Everyday creativity in action.

As leaders, how do we transcend what we think we are *supposed* to do in order to solve problems in new ways, see challenges through fresh eyes and do differently? Keep reading.

Be Creative BODS

A simple cognitive tool I use to help people keep creative approaches top-of-mind is the acronym BODS. It is a set of *four simple questions* that can help us be better problem solvers and deeper thinkers. It is an easy way of prodding us out of default thinking. Here they are:

Better – Is there a *better* way of doing this?

Other – How have *other* people solved similar problems?

Different – What would I see and do differently if I looked at this situation from a completely *different* point of view?

Simple – How can I make this *simple*? Simple is the new smart.

This is a great way of encouraging people to constantly look for improvement opportunities. Imagine what would be possible in a workplace where everyone asked themselves these four questions every day, in everything they did.

Some of the organisations and leaders I have worked with have produced wonderfully colourful and visually engaging posters with these simple questions and put them up around the workspace to keep them top-of-mind. Imagine the impact it would have on an organisation's productivity and outcomes if people at all levels routinely asked themselves these questions.

The Creativity Charter

Another simple way of engaging people on a day-to-day basis in "small c" creativity is to collectively produce a creativity charter. This is where a team agrees on a series of high-level aspirational statements they agree to commit to. Writing a creativity charter can be fun to create and could be used as a good team-building activity. The kinds of statements in a creativity charter could include:

- We agree to be creative BODS and recognise the importance of creativity in our work.

- We will listen to and value the creative ideas of our colleagues without judgment or criticism.

- We will live with the frustrations that come with the implementation of creative solutions.

Spend some time at your next team meeting laying the groundwork for introducing a creativity charter.

A word of caution: I have done this exercise many times with different teams and something I have noticed is that initially, statements can be either too operational or too general. They were neither aspirational nor specifically about creativity.

Here are a few examples of draft statements I helped teams recast to specifically reflect their creativity aspirations.

Before	After
We will harness new technologies, services, practices and research to deliver the best-fit solution for our customers.	We will put our customers first by proactively finding out what they need so that we can creatively harness new technologies, services, practices and research to deliver high-value, innovative, fit-for-purpose solutions.
We will think outside the box.	We will think creatively by constantly seeking solutions that are "outside the box".
We will consult widely, share skills and provide support.	We will consult widely, share skills and provide support with the intention of offering fresh, new perspectives that will result in creative solutions.

Table 2: Creativity Charter Statements

As much as possible, use the language of creativity.

When doing this activity, help your team see the bigger picture of how a simple act like this can contribute to the achievement of much larger and grander goals. For example, a creativity charter keeps creative thinking top-of-mind. This, in turn, leads to a team or workforce that thinks flexibly. This, in turn, leads to a more agile workforce, which can lead to the fulfilment of the strategic goal of becoming an innovative organisation.

KPI of
Innovation in
Strategic Plan

Agile
workforce

Embeds
flexibility of
thought

Creativity
Charter

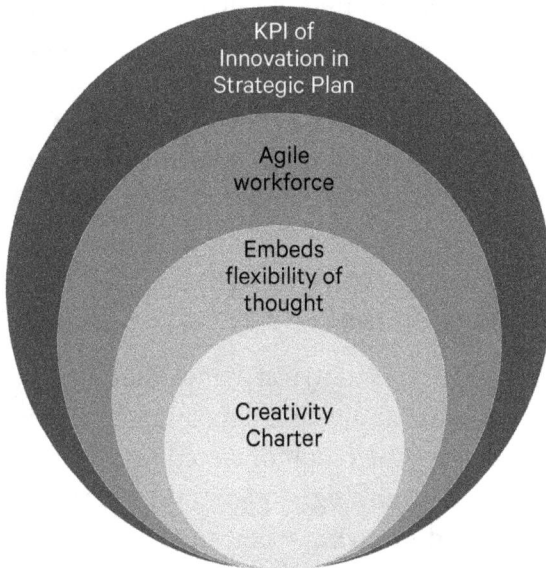

Creativity Promotes a Healthy Workplace

Creative teams have been found to be more efficient with higher levels of staff well-being.[44] This should not surprise anyone when we understand that engaging in creative problem solving helps release the brain chemical dopamine, which makes us feel good and think better. This is why engaging in a creative activity can feel so rewarding. When you have an "ah-ha" moment, your brain receives a squirt of dopamine, which is a pleasant experience. All of us have had the wonderful experience of suddenly getting a flash of insight or inspiration.

There is the famous story of Archimedes, the great ancient Greek mathematician, who had a "eureka" moment that completely carried him away. The story goes that he was grappling with a difficult problem the King had set for him about testing whether or not the King's crown was pure gold or mixed with another metal. As he stepped into the bath, he noticed the accompanying displacement of water and suddenly solved the problem. History tells us that he was so excited about it, he ran naked out of the bathhouse down the streets of Athens yelling, "Eureka! Eureka!"

Thinking creatively challenges us to step *out* of our comfort zone to prevent mental ruts by exercising the brain. This is great for brain health, just as physical exercise is good for the body.

Creative Thinking: An Amalgam of Thought Processes

Creative thinking requires us to use many different kinds of thought processes. It is not just about brainstorming and generating ideas. Creative outcomes are the result of a combination and integration of different kinds of thinking – generating ideas, exploring and evaluating them, and knowing when to switch directions to keep progress on track.

John Cleese[45], comedian, writer, actor and creative thinker extraordinaire, puts it this way:

> "We all operate in two contrasting modes, which might be called open and closed. The open mode is more relaxed, more receptive, more exploratory, more democratic, more playful and more humorous. The closed mode is the tighter, more rigid, more hierarchical, more tunnel visioned. Most people, unfortunately, spend most of their time in the closed mode. Not that the closed mode cannot be helpful. If you are leaping a ravine, the moment of take-off is a bad time for considering alternative strategies. When you charge the enemy machine-gun post, don't waste energy trying to see the funny side of it. Do it in the 'closed' mode. But the moment the action is over, try to return to the 'open' mode – to open your mind again to all the feedback from our action that enables us to tell whether the action has been successful, or whether further action is needed to improve on what we have done. In other words, we must return to the open mode, because in that mode we are the most aware, most receptive, most creative, and therefore at our most intelligent."

The process described above of iteratively moving among different states in response to the needs at hand is akin to the process of design thinking. This is a problem-solving methodology where the problem solver cycles or loops among different kinds of thinking, incorporating progressive outcomes and new information in order to gradually build a solution.

The key message here is that creative thinking is not simply about the process of coming up with new ideas, as is often thought. That is only part of the story. It is also about applying the rigour of exploring the emergent features of a developing solution that are worthy of exploitation, identifying them, extracting them, synthesising them and manipulating them.

Similarly, creative problem solving would be severely frustrated, resulting in inferior solutions, if we didn't apply good evaluative processes to the emerging solution. At some point, the value or usefulness of new ideas must be determined. This is where critical and analytical thinking skills are essential.

The ability to think strategically about the project is also essential in order to reflect on progress, monitor direction and make decisions about whether to change direction and when.

Effective creative problem solving is a whole-brain activity that integrates "left brain"-type activity, represented by logical and analytical thought, with "right brain"-type activity of imagination and creation.

Keeping Thinking Fresh: The Challenge for Innovation Age Leaders

This kind of cognitive activity can feel like really hard work! It is higher-order thinking. By its very nature, creative thinking requires us to forge new mental pathways. Such a process can be discomforting, difficult, messy and frustrating. It creates heavy cognitive load, i.e. a lot of mental effort. It takes us into unchartered territory. When we are busy and stressed, that's the last place we want to go. It's much easier to rely on established patterns of thought and tried-and-true ways of doing things that we know will work. The result? Same ol', same ol'. Default thinking. Boring ideas.

Cognitive tools like BODS, discussed earlier, prompt us into new and fresh ways of thinking and can make the hard work of creative thinking a little easier. There are many others, such as Dr Edward de Bono's Six Thinking Hats®, StrateGEE, SCAMPER and TRIZ.

The good news is that even though creative thinking can feel hard or difficult for many of us, if we make an effort to think differently, we will succeed.

A study at Harvard University[46] found that people who were identified as being innovative spent 50% more time deliberately *trying* to think differently. In other words, they succeeded in being more creative because they put in the effort. That blows out of the water the notion that only people with a certain kind of talent can be creative.

Leaders can help their teams to be more creative by demystifying creativity and encouraging people to persist with generating new ideas to problems, embracing uncertainty and ambiguity, and looking for ways to combine different ideas. Give them "permission", encouragement and reassurance that even if it is difficult, it is worth it.

Viva la Difference!

Great ideas and outcomes come from diverse teams. There is plenty of research showing that teams of diverse thinkers consistently produce outcomes that are better than those produced by teams of experts in the same field. Keep that in mind when putting together project teams. If working on a particularly complex problem, this is almost essential.

For example, it took a team of mathematicians, medical doctors, neuroscientists and computer scientists at Brown University in Rhode Island to create a system that allowed a monkey to move a computer cursor with only its thoughts.[47] Uber's Advanced Technologies Centre in Pittsburg is teaming up with Carnegie Mellon University's National Robotics Engineering Centre to produce a driverless car. And LEGO® was saved from the brink of bankruptcy by collaborating with its loyal customer base to become the "Apple of toys".

So look beyond the boundaries of your team, organisation or agency for people who may be able to add value to your problem-solving procedures. When you assemble a diverse project team that can work together well to solve difficult challenges, what you are doing is *curating talent*. You are sourcing, managing and organising it in a way to facilitate the synergy that leads to creativity.

The best example of this I have ever seen was at the Brisbane GOMA (Gallery of Modern Art). I had taken my daughter to see the "21st Century: Art of the First Decade" exhibition in 2011. For me, the most riveting display of creativity was not the exhibition itself but the space outside. The gallery had set up a huge table, possibly 50 meters long, filled with white LEGO® blocks. Anyone could sit at the table and build whatever they wanted to.

We visited the exhibition not long before it closed, so it had been on display for a few months. During that time, thousands of people, mostly children, had contributed their creativity and talent to build an amazing white LEGO® city. Its beautiful spires, towers and peaks rose majestically from the collection of unassembled white parts still on the table. It was a truly remarkable display of architecture.

On the afternoon we were there, I watched as about 100 children of all ages, shapes, sizes, abilities, skills, cultural backgrounds and varied experiences shared and built on each other's labour to produce a work of art. No supervision was necessary to allocate piles of LEGO®, or to give instructions or issue guidelines about how to play nicely together. The gallery had simply created the conditions and context for diversity and creativity to link arms easily and freely. If only we did more of this in our workplaces.

For me, it was a real vision of the future. I reflected on the fact that many of those young people around the table that afternoon would, during their careers, be working on collaborative projects that could span the globe. They might be part of diverse teams located across numerous international boundaries made up of many different cultures and skillsets. They might even work on major infrastructure projects, building real cities, sourcing knowledge and inspiration from around the world.

Here Are a Few Things We Know About Creativity

Creativity is fueled by association: producing new ideas by combining old ones in new ways (or new ones in old ways). It is more likely to present itself when you are relaxed and not stressed – so soak in a bath, go for a jog, look at the moon, wash the dishes, read some poetry, ride the ferry. Creativity is all colours, not just black or white. There are no right or wrong answers in a creative solution. It is as easy as A-B-C-D: Always Be Connecting the Dots.[48]It's also really hard. And it's messy. Sometimes it is best served when working with others – and sometimes when working alone. You have to figure out which is which for each situation.

Creativity is inconsiderate and will sometimes wake you up in the middle of the night with no more of an excuse than "I was in the neighborhood – thought I'd drop in." You won't find it in your comfort zone. It will be the wind in your sails only after you leave the harbour. Asking lots of questions rings creativity's doorbell. But there's no guarantee it will answer; it depends on what mood it's in.

It is undeterred by failure. It rides with people who explore, experiment and take risks. Daydreaming releases creativity, and so does fantasising – so get yourself an imaginary friend. It loves to hang out where you least expect it, so be prepared for it to jump out at you when you are travelling a new road in the middle of nowhere, out of GPS range and you have no idea where you are. Creativity loves a party, so get some friends together, tell some stories and have a laugh. Its best friend is curiosity – they are almost inseparable. They'll often go for long walks on the beach, arm in arm. They love hanging out together.

The Other Important "C"

Curiosity feeds creativity. One of the hallmarks of creative people is incessant, persistent, unrelenting curiosity; an insatiable desire to know more, explore more, experiment more.

Cultivating curiosity can be simple. Investigate and pursue ideas outside your areas of expertise. Read a magazine that is completely foreign to you. Visit a place you haven't been to before. Drive using a different route. Deliberately seek novelty.

Mihaly Csikszentmihalyi, one of the giants in the field of creativity research, gave us the term *flow*, which has made its way into the popular lexicon to mean being "in the zone". In his landmark book, *Creativity: Flow and the psychology of discovery and invention*[49], Csikszentmihalyi suggests:

1. Try to be surprised by something every day. Be open to what the world is telling you. Life is nothing more than a stream of experiences – the more widely and deeply you swim in it, the richer your life will be.

2.   Try to surprise at least one person every day. Say something unexpected, express an opinion that you have not dared to reveal, ask a question you wouldn't ordinarily ask.

3.   Write down each day what surprised you and how you surprised others. One of the surest ways to enrich life is to make experiences less fleeting so that the most memorable, interesting and important events are not lost forever. Writing them down so you can relive them in recollection is one way to prevent them from disappearing. (P.347)

And why is cultivating curiosity such a worthy investment?

Because curiosity makes for innovative leaders! And why is that?

Because it drives us to look beyond *what is* and asks *what else* or *what if*. It prompts us to re-examine assumptions and wonder about possibilities. It prompts us to transcend preconceptions and see things with a child's openness. It keeps us in enquiry mode, which drives discovery. This inspires fresh thinking and new ideas to stoke the furnace of creativity.

Curious people are destined for the C-Suite. This is the belief of Warren Berger, author of *A More Beautiful Question: The Power of Inquiry to Spark Breakthrough Ideas*[50]. After studying hundreds of the world's leading entrepreneurs and innovators, the common thread he found was that curious enquiry was the starting point for reinventing entire industries.

Tips for Leaders

1. Believe that you and your team members are creative!

2. Value creativity. Give it the respect that it deserves – it will help solve complex problems.

3. Regularly use creativity tools to help people augment their creative-thinking abilities.

4. Put together project teams that are highly diverse.

5. Stoke and feed your curiosity.

In the Presence of Creativity ...

Knowledge is synthesised. People will be able to combine disparate ideas to produce novel solutions to difficult problems to drive innovation.

Talent is optimised. People will use their innate aptitudes and abilities in ways never imagined.

Experience is compound. People will find ways of merging their skillsets to bring deeper solutions to problems.

NOTES

NOTES

META-SKILL #5
ADAPTABILITY

"It is not the strongest of the species that survives, nor the most intelligent. It is the one that is most adaptable to change."

~ Charles Darwin

CHAPTER 7

Meta-Skill #5 Adaptability

"In times of change, learners inherit the earth; while
the learned find themselves beautifully equipped
to deal with a world that no longer exists."

~ Eric Hoffer

The adaptable organisation is populated with leaders who can change to fit new circumstances and can encourage their team members to do so as well. These are people with learning agility: people who want to learn and constantly develop and contribute their skills. As our world and the global economy transform before our eyes, only organisations that can adapt, evolve and innovate effectively will survive. In nature, the organism that can adapt quickly has the maximum chance of surviving and thriving in transitional times. Organisations seeking long-term sustainability in the innovation age also need to develop mechanisms for adaptation. This is more likely to be achieved with an autonomous workforce that is skilled at problem solving and committed to lifelong learning; a workforce that takes responsibility for constantly updating its knowledge, learning new skills and being open to new ways of thinking. The late Alvin Toffler, American writer and futurist, famously said: "The illiterate of the 21st century are not those who can't read or write but those who cannot learn, unlearn, and re-learn."

Keep an eye out for team members who take responsibility for their own learning: those who are self-directed and proactive about their own on-going education, constantly adding to and transforming their skill sets. According to the *Harvard Business Review*[51], these people are likely to become your high performers. These are the people who live by William Ernest Henley's poetic words in *Invictus*: "I am the master of my fate: I am the captain of my soul."

By helping their people to become lifelong learners, good leaders equip them with an important success tool. In the process, the leader also acquires an empowered team of effective thinkers and problem solvers. A good way of doing that is to give people the opportunity to operate in different roles, work with different people across the organisation, and adapt their knowledge and skills for different contexts to solve a variety of problems. The bulk of our adult learning in the workplace happens informally on the job and in collaboration with co-workers.

The Tyranny of Expertise

Being knowledgeable and highly skilled has always been desirable – and still is – but today it is even more important to be *adaptable and flexible* with that knowledge. Being highly skilled implies knowing *how to do something* exceptionally well and being able to do it efficiently and effectively. The down side of that is people can become so good at operating in a particular skill area, they can't *adapt* that knowledge to different kinds of problems. That is the tyranny of expertise.

The best way to guard against this is to continually tackle challenges that require *creativity* rather than *just competence*. Constantly looking for new ways to synthesise knowledge and skills turns a knowledge *expert* into a knowledge *entrepreneur*. That is someone who is able to constantly learn, change and adapt their knowledge to different situations. It is one of the key characteristics of the successful leader of the innovation age.

To quote Shoshana Zuboff, Professor of Business Administration at Harvard Business School, *"Learning is the new form of labor."* It is now our job to be learners.

Let's Not Be Monkeys

I love that well-known story about five monkeys, and some bananas. It is supposedly based on experiments conducted by G.R. Stephenson, a primatologist, but has long passed into the annals of business fables. The original experiment was very different to the form in which it is now told, but it makes a good story. In case you haven't heard it, it goes like this.

A group of scientists placed five monkeys in a cage, and in the middle, a ladder with bananas on top. Every time a monkey went up the ladder, the scientists soaked the rest of the monkeys with cold water. After a while, every time a monkey would start up the ladder, the others would pull it down and beat it up. Eventually, no monkey would dare try climbing the ladder, no matter how great the temptation.

The scientists then decided to replace one of the monkeys. The first thing this new monkey did was start to climb the ladder. Immediately, the others pulled him down and beat him up. After several beatings, the new monkey learned never to go up the ladder, even though there was no evident reason not to, aside from the beatings.

Then a second monkey was substituted and the same thing happened. The first monkey participated in the beating of the second monkey. A third monkey was changed and the same thing was repeated. The fourth monkey was changed, resulting in the same beatings. Eventually, the fifth monkey was replaced as well.

What was left was a group of five monkeys that – without ever having received a cold shower – continued to beat up any monkey who attempted to climb the ladder.

If it was possible to ask the monkeys why they beat all those who attempted to climb the ladder, their most likely answer would be, "It's just how things are done around here." Or, "This is the way we've always done it."

Whatever the source of the story, fact, fiction or fable, we get the point about "received culture".

Innovation age leaders constantly question established practices to avoid becoming trapped in outdated cultural customs. By doing this, they create a workplace where innovation can flourish.

Transcending "Received Culture"

Leading in the innovation age means helping organisations transcend "received culture" to do things differently. A wonderful example of this comes from a government department that had traditionally performed the role of auditor, investigator and regulator of industry in relation to work safety. They evolved their business model to become a partner and collaborator to proactively *avert* crises and *prevent* injury, rather than impose sanctions *after* the event.

The department I refer to is Workplace Health and Safety Queensland in the Department of Justice and Attorney General. By transforming the culture of the work safety regulator from one of compliance control to that of cooperation, collaboration and joint problem solver with business and industry, the incidents of serious work-related injuries are declining across the state.[52] Between 2009 and 2013, injury rates dropped by 25.9% in manufacturing, 30.5% in construction, 15.9% in transport and 16.6% in agriculture.

By transitioning from being predominantly reactive to being proactive, the department's new business model has improved the lives of thousands of workers by helping to create a safer environment in which they can work. The additional flow-on benefit of this new approach is that the insurance premiums businesses pay are reduced, saving them money and making them more competitive. Between 2013 and 2015, data gathered from 38 businesses in high-risk sectors showed that their workers' compensation premiums were reduced between 40% and 60%. In one particular business, the premium reduced by $355,000.

That is not to say they no longer use sanctions at all. That is still part of their role, but it is no longer the primary avenue for improving safety standards.

Flexible Thinking Makes us Adaptable

Innovation age leaders don't get stuck in a default mode of thought but are adaptable enough to see situations from different perspectives.

In 2011, an article appeared in the *Harvard Business Review*, written by Rosabeth Moss Kanter, called "Zoom In, Zoom Out: The best leaders know when to focus in and when to pull back". It was not long after the devastating explosion of the BP oil platform in the Gulf of Mexico that killed 11 people and caused the biggest oil spill in US history. The author analysed the response of the then CEO, Tony Hayward, who was forced to resign a few months after the incident. Kanter concluded that Hayward's undoing was his inability to free himself of the shackles of myopic thinking, missing many opportunities to demonstrate his ability to see the situation from different perspectives.

Such lack of adaptability is dangerous in a world filled with unexpected events. Default positions are rarely effective in a crisis. Hayward needed to see the big picture instead of being preoccupied with the impact of the event on BP's management and, in particular, on himself.

Rather than trying to shift the blame to suppliers, he could have acknowledged the devastation caused by the incident and the intense public consternation. "Even though BP deployed thousands of engineers to contain the spill, he could not, in public, rise above a 10-foot view; it was as if the crisis was his own personal devil."[53] The lack of adaptability in his thinking made a bad situation even worse.

The "T-Shaped" Worker

Interdisciplinarity brings adaptability and flexibility. The "T-shaped" leader is someone who has a deep understanding of their particular field of expertise but is also conversant with, or at least curious about, a broader range of skills from different disciplines.

The term was popularised by Tim Brown, CEO of the innovation and design firm IDEO. He described T-shaped people as having two kinds of characteristics that complement each other: "The vertical stroke of the 'T' is a depth of skill that allows them to contribute to the creative process ... The horizontal stroke of the 'T' is the disposition for collaboration across disciplines."

Creativity is found at the porous boundaries of different disciplines. Hence, the benefit of a well-stocked mind. Combine this with the ability to imagine a problem from another perspective and you have a greater chance of coming up with a genuinely innovative solution.

For example, I recently had a conversation with a senior theatre nurse who told me that her team members were drawing from the field of aviation to improve their professional practice. When it comes to preparation for activities where human lives hang in the balance, pilots understand the importance of having a highly detailed checklist of criteria. Preparation for surgery needs the same approach.

Different Kinds of Adaptability

Let's look in more detail at the capacity that leaders have for adaption. Some leaders may be able to adapt quickly while others need more time. Others are resistant and won't change even if given plenty of time and encouragement.

We began this chapter with the famous quote from Charles Darwin referencing animal adaptability. As with animals, leaders have varying abilities and response rates to change, which affect their survival rates. Let's continue the animal metaphor and use the nexus between *speed* and *capacity to adapt* to look at different leaders' responses to change.

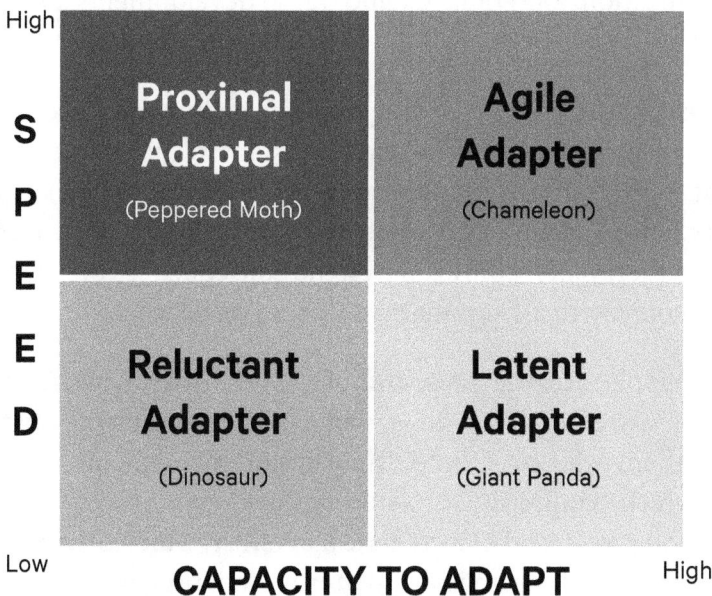

High	**Proximal Adapter** (Peppered Moth)	**Agile Adapter** (Chameleon)
S P E E D	**Reluctant Adapter** (Dinosaur)	**Latent Adapter** (Giant Panda)
Low	**CAPACITY TO ADAPT**	High

The Reluctant Adapter – The Dinosaur

Low adaptability, low speed

The poor dinosaurs are the icons of extinction. The most popular theory is that their environment changed dramatically as a result of a massive meteor strike on Earth. As a result, their habitats were catastrophically disrupted. All life was affected, yet other animals survived. Insects survived, mammals (although scathed) survived, birds survived. Dinosaurs perished. They lacked the ability to adapt.

Our world is in just such a state of disruption right now. We are all living through the metaphorical meteor strike. The rate of change is unprecedented and accelerating – brought about by the advent of the internet, unprecedented access to information, globalised communication, incredible technological developments and a host of other influences.

Anyone who thinks they can keep their head down and "ride it out" is not facing reality. People who are resistant to change are limiting (to put it mildly) themselves, their teams and their organisations. Adapt or die. Organisations such as Kodak, Blockbuster, Borders and Blackberry know only too well the consequences of having too many people with a dinosaur mentality in leadership roles.

These people are the *Reluctant Adapters*. They have learnt to function extremely well in a particular environment that has served them well over time. They resent the changes that face them, which require them to step out of their comfort zone. The adaptation process takes a great deal of effort, which disrupts their well-ordered and established patterns and processes that have proved so efficient in the past.

However, given that the alternative is extinction, they may be persuaded to come on the journey.

The Proximal Adapter – The Peppered Moth

High speed, low adaptability

Peppered moths are famous for their quick adaption to the changing landscape of 19th-century England. In some corridors of the countryside, such as between London and Manchester where coal-burning factories sprang up and blanketed the area in soot, the trees darkened in colour. Due to natural selection, the dark moths survived; the light ones didn't. The white moths fell prey to birds as they were without their camouflage. Within the space of about a decade (a very short time when it comes to evolutionary change), the population of peppered moths had adapted to their environment, shifting from predominantly light coloured to grey and dark-coloured moths.

For the purposes of this model, this represents a rapid adaptation but of a relatively low magnitude. The moths were still essentially the same – just darker in colour. They didn't have to work too hard, from an evolutionary perspective, to survive as a species.

This represents the kind of people who are comfortable with incremental change. They are great at implementing continuous improvement. Provided the change needed is not of a disruptive kind, "peppered moth" leaders are fine with it and can move quickly. They are good at seeing opportunities in process improvements, are results oriented and solve problems efficiently. They are often the backbone of an organisation.

However, they may have trouble envisioning the future from a big-picture, strategic perspective. They find it hard to imagine how their industry may be disrupted in the future. So even though they may be fast action takers, they move forwards in steps rather than leaps.

These people are the *Proximal Adapters*. They can move fast but not far.

The Latent Adapter – The Giant Panda

High adaptability, low speed

The giant panda was in the news recently after being taken off the endangered species list. Genetically speaking, giant pandas are reasonably resilient. They have enough inherent, genetic diversity to be able to adapt to changing environments *given time*. They are more adaptable than other endangered species, such as the Bengal tiger and Namibian cheetah.

The reason they ended up on the endangered list is that the environment changed too fast. However, thanks to some good management on the part of biologists and environmental groups, they are making a slow comeback.

This represents the kind of leader who has the potential to adapt to different contexts given the right support. They have enormous talent and capability but need development and mentoring in order to acquire the confidence to become more agile leaders.

These people are the *Latent Adapters*. They are the slow starters who require significant investment into their development over time. However, in the long run they return the investment exponentially because they are inherently talented and capable individuals.

The Agile Adapter – The Chameleon

High adaptability, high speed

The most well-known characteristic of a chameleon is its ability to adapt to its surroundings and blend in seamlessly and easily. Actually, this is a myth. They certainly change colour, but not *just* in response to the colour of their surroundings. There are a number of factors that influence their colour changes – things such as their mood (calm or angry), territoriality, the temperature of the environment, level of threat from the environment, and even an opportunity to mate.

A recent study has found that chameleons can quickly change colour by adjusting special cells in each layer of their skin. They can change the structural arrangement of the upper cell layer by relaxing or exciting the skin, which leads to a change in colour. Thus, the ability to adapt and change quickly and easily in response to different circumstances or moods is hardwired into their DNA.

The primary motivation is communication rather than camouflage. In other words, they change colours quickly – not only to blend in, but more importantly to send a message to other chameleons or predators.

So to continue the metaphor, the chameleon-type leader is the one who not only adapts quickly to changes in the environment but communicates that effectively to others. Why is the change necessary? What threats and opportunities to the organisation do we need to respond to? Are there emerging collaboration opportunities that could add value to the organisation and its clients or customers?

These people are the *Agile Adapters*. They thrive on change and are energised by it. They understand the dynamics of change and are finely tuned into shifts in the external environment. Such a heightened awareness allows them to lead proactively rather than reactively.

Interestingly, chameleons also shed their skin regularly. *Agile Adapters* are also prepared to reinvent themselves often so that they stay on the leading edge of relevance. They welcome the opportunity to serve in other roles within the organisation and beyond, seeing it as an excellent way to build a wider repertoire of skills and gain new perspectives.

When Meg Whitman was CEO of eBay, she rotated her leadership bench around the organisation. Silos are less likely to occur with that kind of cross-fertilisation of expertise and understanding. It helped them to be more agile leaders.

Encouraging Adaptability

Each quadrant needs different things in order to be more adaptable.

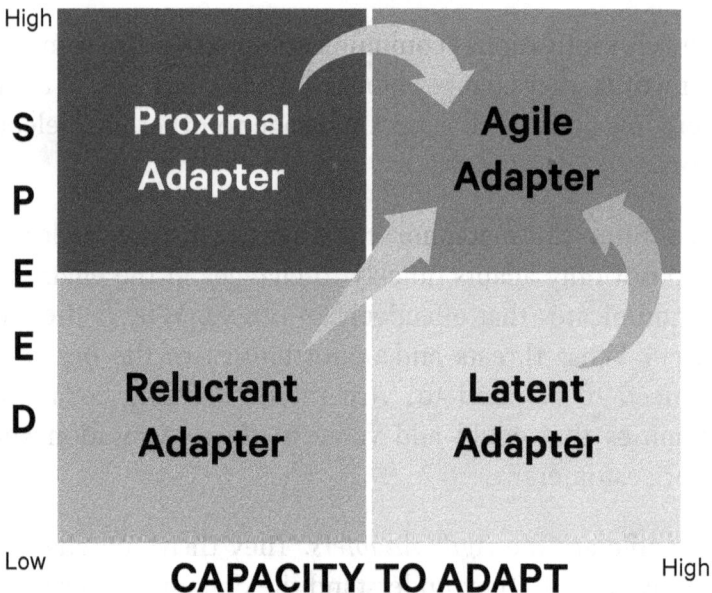

The *Reluctant Adapter* needs inspiration and energy. They need to get out more and see what's happening beyond their immediate environment. *Reluctants* would benefit enormously from going to conferences, networking meetings, industry forums watching TED Talks and reading the latest publications about what is happening in their field and how technology is transforming it. These activities would give them ideas about how they can apply their often deep knowledge base to difficult workplace challenges.

The *Proximal Adapter* needs a bigger vision. They could do with some horizon scanning and use of the STEEPLE acronym to inform their thinking, i.e. what are the Social, Technological, Economic, Environmental, Political, Legal and Ethical factors and considerations that currently impact and will impact the organisation and the industry? They need to ask and answer the question, "How can we be ready for these disrupters?"

The *Latent Adapter* needs a good, progressive development program. This should include working collaboratively with more experienced colleagues on projects of varying complexity. In the process, they will receive informal mentoring, exposure to different kinds of challenges and see things from different perspectives. Such an approach affords them the opportunity to steadily grow their skills, incrementally take on more responsibilities and gain the confidence they need to reach their full potential and eventually step into the role of the agile leader.

The *Agile Adapter* needs a steady stream of opportunities to constantly feed their desire for growth and innovation. They relish the chance to learn from new experiences, so are skilled at transforming and transferring their knowledge across silos to help their organisation and team solve problems in new ways. They need these challenges to keep them energised and engaged.

Adaptation to Technology

Use the technological tools that are at our disposal to augment productivity, communication and creativity. Technological literacy makes us adaptable. The world is filled with so much cool "stuff" that we can appropriate and weave into our lives – professional and personal – to assist us in so many ways. And most of it is freely available!

If you're not sure how to drive a new piece of technology, YouTube it. Just-in-time learning! If one platform or software doesn't work for you for whatever reason, find another one that will. There are plenty out there.

Technology is no longer a novelty – it is the norm. It is not just a "nice to have" or a differentiator, it is core. It pervades every part of our lives. The imperative is no longer to simply have technology, but rather to be clever with how we use it.

Even people who do not consider themselves tech savvy can use assistive technologies to help achieve their goals, improve productivity, make their messages more engaging and communicate in new ways.

I can make that claim with a certain degree of credibility as I have never considered myself a card-carrying "techie". Yet I love the tools I use in my business (and every other part of my life, for that matter) that make it easy to innovate. Just recently, I learnt how to integrate GoToWebinar with Camtasia to make an audio recording of an interview with someone in a remote regional area, which will be repurposed as a podcast.

It took a little experimenting to find the best solution for my purposes. I tried Audacity but could only record my end of the conversation. Camtasia allowed me to rip the soundtrack to turn it into an MP3. Someone reading this is probably thinking, "You can achieve the same outcome more easily using such and such." Sure. But I found my own solution, using platforms I was already familiar with and experimented with combining them in a new way for a new purpose.

Tips for Leaders

1. Being mentally agile will prevent us from becoming stuck in default thinking.

2. Learn something new every day and ask team members to do the same.

3. Look at situations from different perspectives.

4. Identify what kind of adapter you are and create a plan for your development in this area.

5. Experiment with new technology.

In the Presence of Adaptability ...

Knowledge is transformed. Team members will use what they know in new ways by thinking differently.

Talent is expanded. Natural ability is developed through the process of people challenging themselves to experiment with new possibilities.

Experience is matured. By using their skills in different ways, people become more confident operating in multiple contexts.

NOTES

NOTES

_____

_____

_____

_____

_____

_____

_____

_____

_____

_____

_____

_____

_____

_____

_____

_____

_____

META-SKILL # 6
THINKING
STRATEGICALLY

"A leader's job is to look into the future and see the organisation, not as it is, but as it should be."

~ Jack Welch

CHAPTER 8

Meta-Skill # 6 Thinking Strategically

"You've got to think about big things while you're doing small things, so that all the small things go in the right direction."

~ Alvin Toffler

When faced with a challenge, it is tempting to jump to solutions quickly before examining the situation strategically and from different points of view. Today more than ever, leaders need to "think globally and act locally". It is easy to get caught up with the operational demands of the job and lose sight of the big picture. So it is important to constantly challenge assumptions, be future focused and look for opportunities. See the big picture. Ask the big questions. Become aware of how shifts in the external environment could impact your organisation.

A lack of attention to the big picture can result in an unresponsive organisation – and its death knell. It takes a talented leader to shepherd an organisation, a department or team out of the wilderness created by its own hubris or neglect, as illustrated by the following true story.

John became a director of a division within a large state government department. The division was in trouble. A number of its facilities were at risk of losing NATA accreditation. NATA is the National Association of Testing Authorities, which provides independent accreditation of laboratories operating in accordance with relevant standards. NATA accreditation is a prerequisite for providing some services to government. Both private and public sector laboratories require NATA accreditation. So the loss of NATA accreditation for a laboratory effectively means it will need to shut down. In this case, it would have meant a number of the government's own internal facilities would be unable to supply services to their own department.

This situation arose over a period of six to eight years due to a gradual decline in standards brought about by: a lack of skilled staff; poor recruitment decisions; lack of investment in people with technical qualifications; a lack of technical management competencies needed to run such a business; and most of all, a lack of strategic thinking.

The situation was exacerbated by the decentralised nature of the business with a number of locations across regional Queensland. The first decade of the 21st century brought with it an infrastructure boom that tended to concentrate in one particular part of the state – south-east Queensland, along the border with New South Wales and certain coastal hubs. This meant two things. Firstly, there was pressure to deliver in concentrated geographical areas. Secondly, when there was available capacity in other areas that could be utilised in resource-hungry areas in other parts of the state , there was no mechanism by which to redeploy those resources.

The challenge was to get representation for 15 major facilities across a large state to communicate effectively horizontally as well as vertically – from the people who operate on the floor through to the peak body in the state. How was it going to be possible for people to communicate simply so that any issue raised by a practitioner could be investigated by a peak body within the state, without bringing a large number of people to a meeting? In other words, how could issues be resolved quickly and easily without draining resources?

The existing system had given rise to a number of silos of knowledge, experience and practices. There were 12 regions that had their own priorities, styles of management and different ways of doing things. To address these challenges would take a paradigm shift of structure and operational systems. Simply trying to improve the existing system was not an option. Furthermore, as the accreditation and licensing of a number of facilities was at stake, the timeframes in which to achieve this were very short. A resolution was needed in just weeks. Continuous improvement and incremental change was not an option.

Enter strategic thinker extraordinaire John. As director, he took a state-wide approach to rectifying the situation. The first task was to get a consistency of approach across the 27 separate entities around the state, which were running different management and operation systems. All the units were brought under a single system with a single accreditation. This move on its own immediately reduced the management burden and yielded economies of scale that led to higher efficiencies.

By working collegially across the state, bringing the people together into a single "space" not in terms of structure but in terms of *relationships*, John created a relational matrix structure that allowed people to collaborate for better outcomes.

This solution addressed the fact that there was a shortage of leaders, especially technical leaders. There was an imperative to leverage the skills of existing leaders so that they could lead in a broader sense rather than at a single facility.

The new structure promoted good horizontal and vertical communication. It allowed organisational leaders to have a snapshot of the health of the business. Beyond that, it also created an opportunity to resolve not just technical issues but broader business issues, such as workloads, capability and capacity including training and development requirements. The relationships and networks that were developed provided opportunities to shift work and people across the state as needed to meet particular needs. Thus, this restructure produced a genuine state-wide business approach that facilitated the vertical and horizontal sharing of information.

The transformation was achieved in *six weeks* and was *cost neutral.*

The new structure resulted in a number of positive outcomes above and beyond the retention of NATA accreditation. There is now a more holistic way of thinking within the division as a result of the networks they have with people across the state. They have a more flexible and qualified workforce, a culture of continuous learning, open channels of communication through which good ideas and collective learning can be shared for ongoing innovation, and an effective succession plan for the business.

It took a leader with a talent for strategic thinking to save a potentially disastrous situation.

Perhaps the situation wouldn't have needed saving if John's predecessors had taken time out to actively and deliberately engage in big-picture strategic thinking, instead of being so focused on operational issues. One of the greatest traps for leaders is attending to things that are urgent at the expense of the important. They live in a reactive instead of proactive state. They are trapped putting out bushfires without ever doing proactive controlled burning to avoid the bushfires in the first place.

Productivity expert Dermot Crowley in his book *Smart Work*[54] differentiates between a *sense of urgency* versus *senseless urgency*, and *reasonable urgency* versus *unreasonable urgency*. The former is genuine and the latter is fabricated. He says reactivity has come to be accepted as the norm in many workplaces.

Of course, there are tasks that require immediate attention. Of course, we need to respect important deadlines – no question about that. *Real* urgency is a part of every workplace. However, often masquerading as real urgency is false urgency – the things that only seem urgent because someone is shouting about it so loudly, or because we ascribe more importance to a task than it is worth, or because we have been lax in organising ourselves and have created a crisis that could have been averted.

The Strategic Importance of Thinking Time

In our busy workplaces, we thoroughly undervalue this important activity: thinking. This is when we give our brain the space to solve problems, step back and look at things from different perspectives. We need to stop thinking of it as time wasted because we are not actively "doing something".

One CEO of an SME who worked with me instituted an active reflection component in the work day of everyone in his organisation. He asked his employees to schedule 15 minutes every day for thinking time. He invited them to leave the desk, turn off the computer, unhook the phone – whatever it took to give them some head space. They then had to ask themselves questions such as, "What has happened in the past 24 hours that can be improved on? Were there aspects of my own practice that could be better executed? Has anything come to my attention in the past 24 hours that needs to be addressed for business improvement?" Such practices stop people operating in reactive mode and encourage them to think proactively.

This initiative was a "lite" version of Google's well-known *ITO – Innovation Time Out*. Employees were encouraged to spend 20% of their time on innovation projects that arose out of their own interests, passions and expertise. The caveat was that it needed to advance the company's interest in some way. *ITO* was credited with being the source of some of the organisation's most famous innovations, such as AdSense, Gmail, Google Talk and Google News.

Since 2013, Google no longer officially uses the 80/20 rule, but that doesn't mean it has abandoned a commitment to innovation. It has done what all organisations should do – it has simply evolved its processes, choosing to focus on innovation in a different way. Google is a different organisation to what it was 10 years ago. It needs a different innovation architecture. Innovative practices are not set and forget. As an organisation matures and develops, so too must its systems. Just because something worked well 10 years ago doesn't mean it is still the right solution.

The best way to continually make wise course corrections to avoid the icebergs that threaten to sink our innovation efforts is to prioritise strategic thinking.

Beware the Short-Term View

It is tempting to look for quick fixes. They can give us the seductive illusion of achievement without the discipline of thinking strategically. If an organisation is stuck in "quarterly" thinking, it could be jeopardising its long-term corporate health.

In his book *Drive: The Surprising Truth About What Motivates Us*[55], Daniel H. Pink warns about the dangers of myopic decisions. He lists the short-term thinking that triggered the global financial crisis.

> "Each player in the system focused only on the short-term reward – the buyer who wanted a house, the mortgage broker who wanted a commission, the Wall Street trader who wanted new securities to sell, the politician who wanted a buoyant economy during re-election – and ignored the long-term effects of their actions on themselves or others." (P.58)

Short-termism is a concept usually associated with financial decision making where the imperative to show good quarterly earnings overrides everything. But the concept can be applied much more broadly in workplaces that are constantly pressured by time constraints. We can be tempted to make a premature decision for a quick outcome simply so we can cross something off our ever-expanding "to-do" lists. Sometimes that's good – except when it's not.

History is replete with disastrous short-term decisions that desperately needed more strategic thinking.

Thomas Austin introduced rabbits into Australia because he wanted a nice meal. Today, the damage caused by rabbits to agriculture and horticulture in Australia is estimated to be more than $206 million per year.[56] Napoleon Bonaparte invaded Russia in 1812 with one of the largest armies ever assembled, thinking the war would only last a few weeks. It was a disaster and brought about his downfall. In 1982, chocolate manufacturer Mars passed up the chance to be the brand supplying confectionary to Steven Spielberg's *E.T.*, the lovable alien with the very sweet tooth. Competitor Hershey grabbed the opportunity and saw its sales jump 65% in the month the movie was released.

Strategic Thinking ≠ Strategic Planning

The terms "strategic thinking" and "strategic planning" are often used synonymously. But they are not the same. Of course, strategic planning is important, but it is not a substitute for strategic thinking.

Strategic planning is about *analysis*, while strategic thinking is about *synthesis*. Strategic planning is about setting a goal, breaking it down into steps, designing how the steps may be implemented, and estimating the anticipated consequences of each step.

Strategic thinking, on the other hand, is about using intuition, creativity and imagination to formulate an integrated perspective, a vision, of where an organisation should be heading given the shifts in the environment. That requires some big-picture thinking. It requires knowledge of local trends, as well as the megatrends that will inevitably wash across the organisation. The only way the organisation will be buoyant in such an environment is if the leaders look *up* from their day-to day-activities.

So the next time all the leaders of your organisation get together, rather than just focusing on the goals for the next quarter or the next 12 months, consider some of these issues and the impact they will have on your current core business. How will your organisation need to reinvent or reposition itself and re-engineer internal roles and structures in the face of these megatrends? Here are a few:

- The rise of "Chindia." The world's economy is shifting from west to east and from north to south – predominantly Asia. The coming decades will see one billion people in Asia transition out of poverty and into the middle-income bracket. By 2030, Asia will represent 66% of the global middle-class population.[57] For those of us living in Australia, this has huge implications that will impact nearly every industry – education, tourism, investment, immigration, manufacturing.

- Urbanisation. Fifty percent of the world's population now lives in cities, with 1.5 million people being added to this total every week. How are the housing and food industries, government infrastructure and services, and energy providers adapting to this? How do we make these cities liveable and sustainable?

- Technological and digital disruption. In Chapter 1, I shared the statistic that by 2020 technological knowledge will double every 73 days. We are already living in a digital world. Technology is increasingly embedded in every part of our lives. This transformation brings with it a range of threats and opportunities. It raises cyber security and privacy concerns, while at the same time offering the opportunity for transformative levels of service.

- Rise of the "access" economy. Otherwise referred to as the sharing economy, collaborative consumption or peer-to-peer business, this is where people gain direct, easy (and often relatively inexpensive) access to goods and services previously inaccessible to them. Uber, Airbnb, eBay, Amazon, SnapGoods, Couchsurfing, DogVacay, TaskRabbit, Getaround, Udemy, Lyft and a host of other platforms are largely accessible via smartphone apps. It's a whole new way of servicing peoples' needs. Traditional service providers, be they businesses or government agencies, teetering on the brink of the innovation gap need to rethink their methods.

- Constant connectivity. Traditional communication channels have limited reach compared to the connectivity offered via social media, smartphone apps and online platforms. In July 2016, Turkey's President Recep Tayyip Erdogan contained a coup via *facetime*! One of the main reasons the coup failed was because the rebels were using an outdated strategy and failed to take into consideration the power of social media.

There is a massive amount of information available on all these topics. I have just curated a few of the more pervasive megatrends. Each organisation, depending on its core business, will be impacted by a diversity of trends. For example, sporting groups are facing a decline in organised sports as people increasingly fit their exercise into busy schedules and opt for non-organised activity. Associations in general are finding that fewer people are joining, and charities and community groups are facing steady declines in volunteers. Point being, do your leaders come to strategic thinking days already armed with this knowledge, ready to apply it to the challenges facing your organisation and industry?

A great way for people to hit the ground running on strategic thinking days is for leaders to be STEEPLE-ready before they arrive. STEEPLE stands for **S**ocial, **T**echnological, **E**conomic, **E**nvironmental, **P**olitical, **L**egal, **E**thical. These leaders have already researched and understand how any (or all) of these factors impact the organisation's core business. They already know what's on the horizon in relation to these considerations and what effect will have on what the organisation does and how it does it. The conversation can then start at a much deeper level.

Look At Me, Look At Me!

Often, the root cause of the busyness syndrome is a deep insecurity. People are trying to impress others by their appearance of hard work, their indispensability, their apparent dedication and commitment to the organisation.

In 2002, the *Harvard Business Review* published an article called "Beware the Busy Manager".[58] The authors observed that busyness can be a function of workplace culture.

> "Indeed, many companies encourage, and even reward, frantic activity. We have noticed, for example, that in organisations whose CEOs and senior executives exhibit aggressive, unreflective behaviour, it's far more likely that other managers will be distracted."

Busyness is a pervasive and insidious organisational disease that cunningly robs organisations of their ability to innovate. It saps the desire to try new things and surreptitiously squanders the most precious resource available to a leader: time. It camouflages itself as pretend productivity and gives people the delusion that all their frenetic activity is worthwhile. All the while nothing really important is actually getting done: innovation that will increase productivity; collaboration that will improve services; problem-solving that will resolve complex issues.

If you are the kind of person who needs to see things in their diary before they do them, then schedule thinking time. Put it in your diary if that's what works for you. Treat that time as sacred. Let your team know that it is the most important work you do – and encourage your team members to do it, too. Without it, leaders end up living in "maintenance mode" rather than "future focus" mode.

Unless we consciously take time out to think strategically, we are doomed to become mired in "business as usual" mode. That kind of thinking traps us in short-sighted decision making. We sacrifice the important for the urgent.

We can't be *strategic leaders* without engaging in *strategic thinking.*

Busyness and "strategicness"[59] are constantly at odds. It's hard to think strategically, take a big-picture view and find deep, rather than shallow, solutions to pressing problems when one is overcommitted, distracted and unfocused. Dr Jason Fox in his book *How to Lead a Quest: A handbook for pioneering executives*[60] refers to the phenomena of busyness as the "Curse of Efficiency". It gives the delusion of progress without actually delivering meaningful progress: "Thanks to the Curse of Efficiency, our time for *thorough* thinking is often crowded out by fast thinking."

The irony is that when we engage in the most important work there is, we look like we're not working. In fact, we look like we're slacking off because we're not rushing around desperately. Rather, we're sitting and thinking. Or, in the case of Leonardo da Vinci, *lying down* and thinking. He had a bed in his studio that he regularly used for time-out thinking. When patrons accused him of wasting time, he said, "If I don't do this, you don't get the work."

In May 2015, *Time* magazine published an article with the provocative title, "You Now Have a Shorter Attention Span Than a Goldfish"[61]. It was reporting on a study conducted by Microsoft Corp., which showed that people lose concentration after eight seconds! The humble goldfish supposedly has an attention span of nine seconds. The title claim was made based on data that showed 77% of people aged 18 to 24 responded "yes" when asked, "When nothing is occupying my attention, the first thing I do is reach for my phone."

The title is misleading but makes for good "clickbait". Obviously, we have much longer attention spans than eight seconds when engaged in some activity. Presumably, you are not reading this book one sentence at a time. But when given the opportunity to be still and *think*, many people now habitually reach for their smartphone instead. After all, there are text messages to send, emails to check, pictures to upload, vines to watch or edit, posts to like or update, cute cat videos to view, headlines to read and a myriad other activities that keep us informed and engaged in our constantly connected world.

In an environment filled with multiple screens and devices vying for our attention, the capacity to engage in sustained internal thought of any other kind – reflective, creative, strategic – is one that needs to be consciously and deliberately nurtured.

What can you do less of, or delegate more of, to give yourself sustained strategic thinking time?

Create the Space

Much of my work in innovation involves working with small groups of leaders through a mentoring process. One of the most common comments I hear is, "It is so valuable to be able to take a step back and get a different perspective on what's happening in the workplace."

Indeed, many issues that seem as difficult to unravel as Gordian's Knot[62] are tamed as a result of stepping out of the situation and getting a different perspective. A meta-perspective. Without this, leaders inevitably become mired in micro-management practices.

Generally speaking, leaders spend far too much time micro-managing behaviours and events that *constitute* the workplace culture and far too little time concentrating on the *meta* issues that *create* the culture.

One manager I worked with from a university in Brisbane told me he had been trying to get to a student engagement project for three years! But he was so *busy*, it never got done. Potentially, the project had a high strategic value. But it wasn't until he was able to give himself permission to step away from the busyness that he could make it happen. And he achieved his outcome in a relatively short timeframe.

There is a well-known fable about a woodcutter straining to saw down a tree. He is working hard but making little progress. A stranger passing by watches for a while and says to the woodcutter, "You are exhausted! And not making headway. Stop for a moment and sharpen your saw. Then you will be able to cut the tree faster and with less effort."

The woodcutter replies, "I don't have time to stop and sharpen the saw. I'm too busy."

When was the last time you sharpened your saw?

Tips for Leaders

1. Think global, act local. See the big picture even while attending to details.

2. Value the importance of thinking and reflection time for bringing increased productivity and higher-quality outcomes.

3. Consciously step out of operational mode, where you are caught up in reactive behaviour, or busy mode and step into strategic mode so you can give attention to the *important*, not just the urgent.

4. Be aware of the dangers of short-term thinking.

5. Schedule time for strategic thinking.

In the Presence of Thinking Strategically ...

Knowledge is recontextualised. Taking a step back and seeing the big picture enables us to find ways of applying our knowledge in different situations.

Talent is revitalised. By avoiding becoming stuck in operational mode we can stay fresh, thereby preventing ourselves from going stale.

Experience is repurposed. Allowing ourselves the head space to think helps us find new and different ways of using our skills.

NOTES

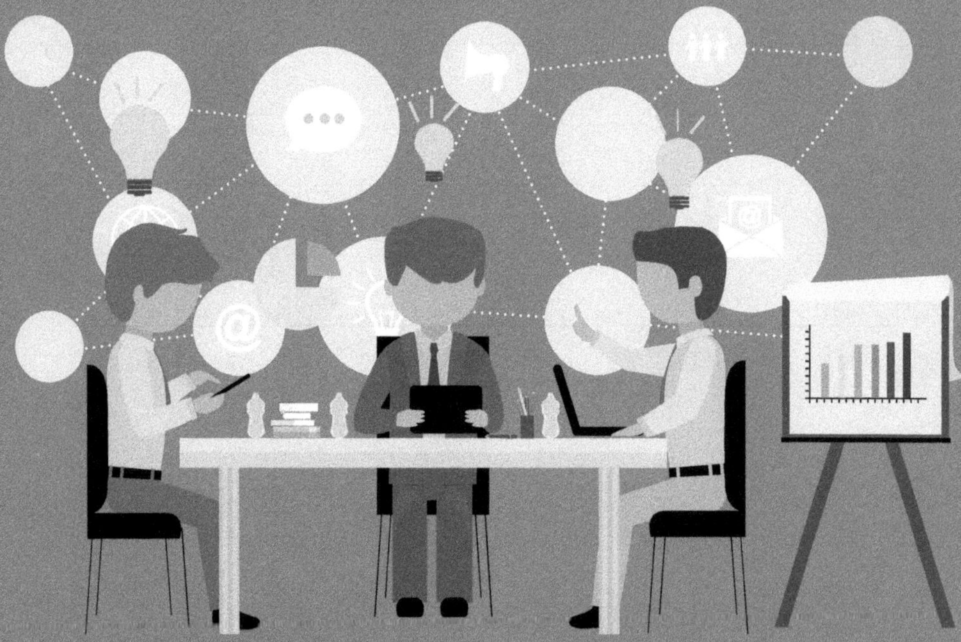

META-SKILL # 7
ENGAGEMENT

"The leaders who work most effectively, it seems to me, never say
'I'. And that's not because they have trained themselves not to
say 'I'. They don't think 'I'. They think 'we'; they think 'team'. They
understand their job to be to make the team function. They accept
responsibility and don't sidestep it, but 'we' gets the credit ... This
is what creates trust, what enables you to get the task done."

~ Peter Drucker

CHAPTER 9

Meta-Skill #7 Engagement

"As a leader, you should always start with where people are before you try to take them to where you want them to go."

~ Jim Rohn

In a call centre for a major American bank, there were vastly different levels of productivity among the teams. Some teams seemed to be able to handle calls so much faster. Why? They were all operating from the same script, working the same number of hours with the same equipment. Turns out the difference was how they took their coffee breaks.

Managers of the poor-performing teams had scheduled *individual* coffee breaks for team members *to cut down on socialising.* Consequently, there was little sense of community or opportunity for knowledge sharing. When they changed that practice to having team-wide coffee breaks, and encouraged people to share ideas not just about work but life in general, productivity skyrocketed. When the practice was implemented across all the call centres for that bank, profits rose by $15 million.

This research was done by MIT's Human Dynamics Laboratory. Director Alex Pentland has also investigated how ideas and information spread through an organisation. He and his team have used "collaboration wearables" to analyse the correlation between idea flow, collaboration, information exchange and performance. In an article called "Betting on People Power" published in *Scientific American Mind*[63], he reports on findings that show a team's success had little to do with its collective IQ or even motivation; rather, it was about how communication and engagement were optimised within the group.

Engagement! Get this right and you increase productivity, decrease "presenteeism" and deliver great outcomes. Get this wrong and you are constantly frustrated!

Engaged employees are more productive, innovative and satisfied. Organisations with engaged employees are more profitable and effective. Engaged people give more discretionary effort, are more loyal and deliver higher levels of customer service. Engagement levels are an accurate predictor of organisational success. Yes, I'm stating the obvious. Yet research from around the world suggests that in most organisations, less than 30% of employees are *actively engaged*. In the United States, Gallup estimates that disengaged employees cost the US economy between $450 billion and $550 billion each year in lost productivity.[64]

It is widely acknowledged that the two critical factors in an employee's level of engagement is the quality of their relationship with their manager and the quality of their relationships with their colleagues. When people leave a job, often what they're *really* doing is leaving the people.

Here are a few suggestions for increasing engagement:

1. Generate ownership and buy in through "co-creation". People support what they help create.

2. Help employees to understand and appreciate *why* they do what they do and not just what they do. People are looking for *purpose.* The workplace that provides purpose is more likely to

have engaged employees. Pulitzer Prize-winning author Studs Terkel said, "Work is about a search for daily meaning as well as daily bread, for recognition as well as cash, for astonishment rather than Torpor."

3. People are more engaged when they feel connected to their colleagues. Get them talking to each other. More on that soon.

4. Provide people with the opportunities to improve and develop their skills and capabilities so they can advance their careers.

5. People become more engaged when they feel that their leaders have a genuine interest in them. So if you are a *task focused* leader, take an interest! Put your Emotional Intelligence on steroids and actively listen.

That last point was something I had to learn when I first started my consulting business after leaving academia. That was more than 10 years ago. At the time, I had a lovely PA who was quite chatty. I'm not much of a chatter. If you are familiar with the DISC profile, you'll know what I mean when I say I was a high "C", which stands for Conscientious as it relates to that particular tool. Such people just want to get on with it without too much fuss, small talk or distraction. Talking about what people did on the weekend is generally not high on their list of priorities. So I would have to put a Post-It note on my computer to remind me to ask Cheryl about her weekend and what her family was up to. I had learned that if I stopped and had a chat for a bit, everything else went more smoothly.

After 10 years in business, my DISC profile looks different. I have learnt that it is precisely that kind of communication that makes the world go 'round and creates happy workplaces. My current Executive Manager has a very different boss.

Engagement is not a set-and-forget process. Engaged team members don't magically stay that way indefinitely without ongoing support and input. As with any relationship, ongoing nurturing is required.

Let's Do Lunch

Collaboration facilitates engagement (and by extension productivity) because it opens the channels of communication, creates connection and builds relationships.

Sometimes, seemingly small initiatives can bring exponential results. For example, one emerging leader, Janine, from a regional government department, recently undertook a project that she called *Collaborative Conversations*. The intention was simply to encourage the people in her area to form deeper relationships with each other to build a more cohesive team culture and look for collaboration opportunities.

Each week, people would go for a coffee with a different person. She formalised it by creating a schedule so that people knew who their coffee partner was for the duration of the project, which lasted for a couple of months. She also provided a loose framework for the conversations to encourage people to engage in deeper discussions and dialogues.

Initially, there was not universal enthusiasm for the project; indeed, it would be fair to say there was even some cynicism about it. However, as people started getting to know each other and formed deeper relationships at work, a wonderful thing happened. A new spirit of collegiality began to diffuse the area. People who had worked side by side with each other for years suddenly discovered that they had many things in common they didn't know about. And they also had many interesting differences that were also a source for celebration.

A whole new level of respect and empathy has resulted in the entire team delivering improved customer service, a willingness to proactively assist colleagues and share information, and actively collaborate.

Apart from being able to tap into each other's work-related technical expertise, they are now having much more fun together.

When I spoke with Janine recently, she told me that the team was planning a lunch – with a difference. Turns out that one team member is an expert in Japanese cooking. Everyone pitched in for the purpose of buying the ingredients and the Japanese cooking expert is preparing a wonderful Japanese banquet for the team. That would never have happened a few months earlier.

The success of the project was reflected in the fact that the team has elected to rerun the program. What's more, a number of other regional offices that heard about the success of the project are now running it with their teams.

There is plenty of research to show that when teams have the opportunity to socialise and develop a group identity, it boosts productivity and resilience.

Team leaders have found different ways of adapting this process for their workplaces. One went so far as to create little laminated cards to hand to team members with the names of their coffee buddies for the week. Another one put a red-and-white-checkered tablecloth on a table in the courtyard to create the atmosphere of an Italian alfresco experience. Another built it into his induction process for new team members so they could feel welcomed by their colleagues from the beginning.

One manager said to me that the ritual of people pairing off regularly for coffee had increased the amount of proactive knowledge sharing within her area to the extent that she was noticing that projects were coming to fruition more quickly.

In the Department of Natural Resources and Mines, two managers – Emily and Brent – went for their collaborative conversations and quite by accident solved a problem in an unexpected way. Emily was working on a project to geo-reference their historical map collections. She was getting that massive job done predominantly through crowdsourcing. During the course of the conversation, they hit upon a way of including the area of the business and their network that dealt with native title. That group has a strong interest in the geo-referencing of historical maps in order to help with native title cases. So by collaborating with them, Emily and Brent were able to expedite the immense job. The native title group even took over project managing the work, developing the procedure to get the historical maps from the museum geo-referenced. I caught up with Brent, who was just about to retire, and he said to me, "It was probably the best 15 minutes of my working life because of the remarkable benefits that came from it. We were able to connect the dots coming from two completely different directions."

Sometimes the simplest of activities can yield the greatest rewards. Simple is the new smart!

Invoke the FOMO Principle

FOMO stands for **F**ear **O**f **M**issing **O**ut. When people see new initiatives working well, generating results and enthusiasm, and people having fun and enjoying themselves – they want to get on board. It's human nature.

So one of the fundamentals of engaging people in any innovation initiative is to make it "sexy". By that I mean make it look like fun. Make it appealing, rather than just hard work. Then people will step onto the innovation bus voluntarily. Without doing this, you could end up like Sisyphus, pushing the proverbial boulder uphill only to have it roll back down, thereby never making progress. FOMO.

Tracey joined my mentoring program when she stepped into a senior leader role with a group of 14 clever, experienced engineers. She was determined to do things differently, which she did. Her story is below. When I asked her what she was most proud of, she said that it was that people were having *fun* at work. She said she loved the fact that now when she walked through the workspace, she could hear people laughing, see them smiling. They were enjoying their work and each other's company. They were engaged!

How did she achieve that?

Firstly, Tracey started with getting everyone on the same page via a team charter where the group collectively identified their key values and principles. That exercise on its own was revelatory and took them on quite a journey together. By the end of that exercise, the team members were so pleased and proud of what they had come up with that they creatively designed their charter and proudly displayed it around their workplace – some people even had it as their screen saver on their computers.

Secondly, Tracey opened the channels of communication by asking all team members to give an eight to 10-minute presentation to their colleagues about their work history, previous experience and anything else they wanted to share, such as hobbies and interests. They could use whatever mode they wanted – story-telling, a PowerPoint presentation, interpretive dance (no one did that). Knowing that this initiative may not be universally welcomed because people weren't used to sharing information beyond their immediate work context, she spoke to team members individually to garner support and sound out objections. It was a smart move. People who may have originally been resistant appreciated being consulted.

Over the course of a few weeks, people took turns to share their stories. The creativity it unleashed was wonderful. One person wove a home movie throughout their story.

What they discovered about each other was utterly amazing!

People had other degrees (including Masters and PhDs), some from areas unrelated to their current work requirements. They had worked in incredibly interesting places all around the world, from major global cities such as London, Bahrain and Hong Kong to places that were off the beaten track, such as East Timor, Vanuatu and Swaziland. One team member had had three children in three different continents.

Some people discovered that they had lived and worked in remote regional Queensland at the same time and even lived near each other. There were lots of interesting intersections that people had been unaware of. There was a broad array of past experience that people brought into the team that everyone had been oblivious to – from having served in the army in Iraq to being a UN volunteer for natural disasters, to being a marketing consultant with celebrities.

People discovered that their colleagues had passions for cooking, jazz dancing, motorbikes, surfing, pistols, martial arts, played musical instruments, belonged to a band. Everyone was dumbfounded when the quietest, most gentle team member revealed he had a black belt in karate and wrestling, and had won high-level competitions. People looked at each other through a new pair of eyes after this exercise.

Thirdly, she revamped team meetings. She did not want them to be boring one-way talkfests with no proactive knowledge sharing. But rather than decree how the new-look team meetings would operate, she asked the team members themselves to come up with ways to restructure the meetings to make better use of their time together. People support what they help create. So now they rotate the chair of each meeting so that everyone has a chance to lead. They have only have 10 minutes of "management speak" and spend much more time on knowledge sharing.

Every month, they pool their collective knowledge resources and together engage with a particular engineering issue using the BODS (Better Other Different Simple) principle. Sometimes they play a relevant TED Talk, then analyse what they can learn from it and how they can transfer that learning to their professional practice. They regularly share learnings from project issues, which means that their professional and technical knowledge is growing fast.

And to top it all off, they are having fun!

Let's Start at the Very Beginning – A Very Good Place to Start

Many organisations miss the prime opportunity to engage employees from the outset with poor corporate on-boarding and orientation practices. One manager in a government department once told me she was nearly ready to quit after her first week because of the frustration she felt when she came on-board. Her passwords hadn't been organised, which meant she couldn't access the intranet, which had all the vital information she needed. She wasn't given an organisational structure so she didn't have a clear understanding of who was who or where she sat in the organisation. There was no formal reception to meet team members. She felt isolated and unwelcomed and did no productive work for a week.

If that was not an isolated occurrence and was repeated even just a few times, imagine the cost to this department. Apart from having a disengaged employee, they were paying someone to do little more than keep a seat warm for more than a week. Worse still, what if she had, in fact, left? There would have been the additional cost of recruiting again for the position.

Done well, the on-boarding process can create strong advocates for the organisation and powerful brand ambassadors.

Perhaps one on the most successful induction programs of all time is used by the New Zealand national rugby team, generally known as the All Blacks. They are the only international team to have a winning record against every nation they have played.

When a player joins the All Blacks, they are given a small book bound in black leather. The first page shows a jersey from 1905, known as "The Originals", followed by jersey after jersey of historic All Black teams up to the present day. Then the inductee is reminded of the principles that underpin the ethos of the team, and past heroes who have exemplified these values The remaining pages are blank, waiting for the new member to write their own story and create their own legacy.

As the induction continues. Emphasis is placed on the development of the whole person and the significance beyond the field of wearing the jersey.

Employee Experience

Successful organisations focus on meeting customer needs and creating customer experience. This is what generates raving fans and brand advocates. Apple was very good at this. When I bought my first Apple product – the original iPad – at the Apple store, I received a standing ovation as I walked out. In-store customers clapped as well, getting caught up in the hype of the moment. Perhaps not everyone would have welcomed such attention; I can imagine some may have cringed. Not me. It certainly created a different kind of shopping experience.

But today it is not just customer experience that is crucial: just as important is *employee experience.*

Richard Branson is famously quoted as saying, "If you look after your staff, they'll look after your customers. It's that simple."

The role of HR departments is evolving from "managing" human resources to creating employee experience. It represents a shift away from the basic assumption of "people work here because they *need* to" towards "people work here because they *want* to". People want to work in environments where they feel valued, respected and satisfied; where they have a sense of purpose and commitment; and where they are mentally stimulated with opportunities to develop themselves.

HR managers now find themselves in a "war for talent". Technology platforms such as LinkedIn have made it much easier to steal or head-hunt talent from other organisations. The power has shifted from the employer to the employee. Talented people are in demand and keeping them engaged is the key to building a robust and energised workforce ready to meet the challenges of the innovation age.

Smart organisations give employees the opportunity to "sculpt" their jobs to provide greater job satisfaction and engagement. It reverses the traditional notion that the employee has to fit into the job. Rather, the job profile is designed around the employee's interests.

When people feel valued and respected at work, they are more likely to be productive, happier and engaged. It seems obvious! Yet a study of nearly 20,000 employees around the world found that 54% of them claimed they didn't regularly get respect from their leaders[65]. The cost of this to the organisation is massive! Employees are less creative and innovative; customer relationships are damaged, as well as the reputation of the organisation; the quantity and quality of work decreases; productivity suffers; and turnover increases.

Incivility has a negative effect on brain function – whether you are the recipient or happen to witness it. Research has shown that just seeing a leader demonstrate rudeness reduces the performance of the observers in routine and creative tasks. In other words, performance decreases on cognitive tasks.[66] To put it in the vernacular, we can't think straight in an environment of disrespect.

Successful leaders of the innovation age are committed to creating positive employee experiences. They are role models of civility in their own behaviour and nip in the bud any disrespect team members show towards each other. The cost of not doing so is too great.

Engaging People in Innovation

In Shakespeare's immortal words, "All the world's a stage, and all the men and women merely players. They have their exits and entrances." Every workplace has different "players" who give and take in different ways. Each has their own unique way of either adding or subtracting value depending on their level of skill (capacity/ability) and will (motivation/desire). This is the case when it comes to engaging with innovation in the workplace. When we look at the nexus between these two factors we get the following quadrant model, which gives insight into different kinds of engagement with workplace innovation.

High

S	**Innovation Conscript** *Has the capacity to innovate but doesn't want to*	**Innovation Champion** *Highly skilled and motivated to innovate*
K		
I		
L	**Innovation Cynic** *Neither can innovate nor wants to*	**Innovation Candidate** *Lacks skill but is keen to learn how to innovate*
L		

Low   **WILL**   High

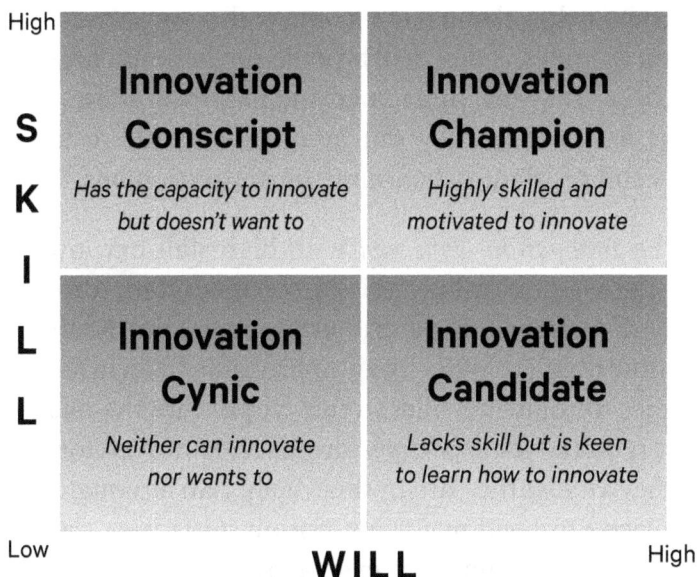

Let's start with the *Innovation Candidate*. These are the new recruits – often graduates. Like the season of spring, they are a breath of fresh air, full of promise and potential. They have high levels of energy and motivation but low skill levels. They are enthusiastic, keen, eager to learn and add value. The limiting factor of their performance is simply that they lack experience; they are "green" and need to spend some time learning the industry and the business. They may experience high levels of anxiety if they feel more is being asked of them than they can deliver because they don't yet have the necessary skills and experience. So the wise leader will check in with them frequently.

Going clockwise, next is the *Innovation Cynic* with low levels of skill and will. Unlike spring, they are the "winter of discontent"[67]. These people have typically neglected their professional learning and development and now find that they have been left behind. They have allowed themselves to become obsolete in a world where that is tantamount to cardinal sin. Therefore, they find it difficult to embrace the further changes that come with the implementation of innovation as it means they will be even further out of their depth. It's a catch-22. They feel threatened and may even adopt a "victim" mentality. As a result, they can be openly hostile to innovation initiatives and resistant to boarding the innovation bus.

Next is the *Innovation Conscript* with high skill but low will. To continue the seasons analogy, this person is autumn, "drows'd with the fume of poppies", as described by poet John Keats.[68] These people know their job well – they've probably been in their role or similar roles for quite a while, so they appreciate the nuances and subtleties required for expert performance. However, for whatever reason, they've lost the "fire in their belly". So although they may be well placed to head major innovation initiatives, they are not motivated to do so. Some may even go so far as to undermine and subtly sabotage the innovation efforts of their team.

Finally, we have the *Innovation Champion* with high skill and high will. These productive people bring "the summer sunshine and great bursts of leaves growing on the trees"[69]. They bring energy and momentum to the business, organisation or team. These are the people who have kept themselves on the leading edge of their chosen fields. They are well informed and up with the latest research and technological developments. They are excited by the work they do and want to experiment with ways of doing things differently for even better outcomes. They are enthusiastic, dedicated and creative. They identify themselves as innovators and are at the top of the Levels of Cognisance model discussed in Chapter 5. Because they can't help themselves, they may even fly under the radar to implement innovation if they are working with a manager who is a *Conscript* or a *Cynic*.

How do we engage people in each quadrant? Let's look at each in turn and what they need to get fired up for innovation.

But before we do that, let's acknowledge that when we are dealing with people, we are working with a complex system. There are no guarantees or hard and fast rules. Nothing is set in concrete. Often, approaches we assume are ideal solutions for a situation can be completely ineffectual. People move around the quadrants depending on what is happening in other parts of their lives, the nature of the work they are doing or the prevailing politics or dynamics in the workplace.

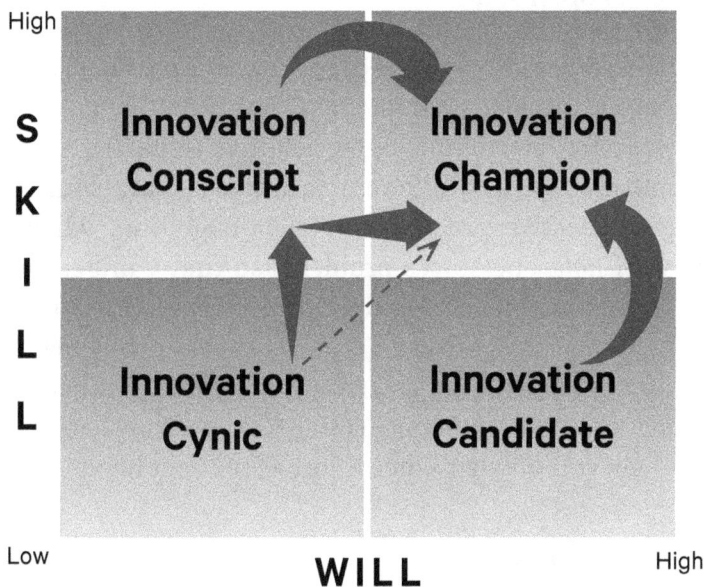

Engaging the Candidate

The *Candidate* needs an on-going program of learning and development with plenty of opportunity to apply that into their role. They benefit enormously with on-the-job mentoring and being teamed with more experienced team members to whom they can serve as "cognitive apprentices".

Cognitive apprenticeship is a time-honoured method of skill development. In the days before formal schooling, learners learnt by watching and operating alongside a "master" – perhaps a parent, an elder or a craftsman who explicitly demonstrated and explained the process (modelling), let the learner have a go with varying degrees of help and support (scaffolding), stepped back and let them loose with it (fading), and finally offered guidance and mentoring as needed to grow their expertise (coaching). For centuries, this was how people learnt what they needed to – whether it was planting crops, weaving garments, carving stone or a multitude of other skills.

In the 21st-century workplace of the innovation age, cognitive apprenticeship is making a comeback. It is a particularly relevant methodology for developing highly adaptive skills that are readily transferable to new and different problem-solving situations. It encourages reflective practice and meta-cognition, which is an awareness of *how* one solves problems so they can get better at doing it. And it enables authentic, contextualised, in-situ learning – which simply means learning to solve real problems, in real time, for real people. It's a great way to develop *Candidates* into *Champions*. The case study in Chapter 5 about progressing people through the levels of cognisance is just as relevant here.

Engaging the Cynic

The *Cynics* needs motivation *and* skill development. Unfortunately, they are not always open to being "mentored" by a more expert team member because chances are they've actually been in the job longer and therefore see themselves as the more senior person.

Realistically, it is unlikely that a *Cynic* will move into the *Champion* quadrant directly. If you can move them into the *Conscript* quadrant with some good training or professional development, you've done well. Moving up is easier than moving across, which requires an attitudinal change.

The most effective way of engaging the *Cynic* is to identify their WIIFMs. This stands for **What's In It For Me**. Work with them to help them see the benefit for them of developing their skills and participating in projects that fire them up – without being accusatory. Give it time.

But what happens when you, as a leader, have tried everything you can think of to re-engage a disengaged employee and it just doesn't work? What happens when you have everyone on the innovation bus ready to go and one person won't get on board? What do you do?

We have to be careful that we don't let one disengaged person suck up all our time and energy. There can be a multitude of reasons for why someone is disengaged – just make sure it's not *you*. There's an old saying, "employees don't leave companies, they leave managers".

One solution suggested by Jim Collins in *Good To Great and the Social Sectors*[70] is to go ahead and change the culture around the *Cynic* so that they feel as though they are "viruses surrounded by antibodies and self-eject". Some people will never come on-board.

Sometimes people are unhappy and disengaged because they are in the wrong job. Finding the right niche for people is worth the effort. One manager recently told me of her experience with a very dissatisfied team member. She was unenthusiastic, withdrawn and disengaged (the team member, not the manager). Finally, the manager had a very open conversation with her and said, "I'd love to support you to find another position to which you are more suited, where you can be more engaged and motivated by your work."

Initially, the team member was quite surprised – but admitted that she wasn't happy in her job. The manager's offer was entirely genuine and motivated from a place of authentic care. So she worked with her team member to find another position more suited to her skillset within the organisation. She supported her through the process of application and interview – and she got the job. Now, she is happy, productive and thriving.

Engaging the Conscript

Conscripts can often be re-engaged by finding a pet project that reignites their fire. They need inspiration, purpose and motivation. Their high skill levels may be put to good use by asking them to mentor a *Candidate* to help develop technical and professional capacities. This does require good judgment, as the last thing you want is an enthusiastic candidate being infected with negativity. But if the pairing is right, then the *Conscript* finds a new purpose and the *Candidate* finds a new source of knowledge. Perhaps some of the *Candidate's* enthusiasm will flow to the *Conscript*.

Conscripts don't usually volunteer. The best way to get them on board with an initiative is to approach them privately. Have a chat rather than put the call out.

Let them know that you believe in them and that their skills and talents matter. Show them appreciation. Rosabeth Moss Kanter, professor at Harvard Business School, observed through her research that there is a significantly higher volume of "thank-yous" in high-innovation companies.

Engaging the Champion

Champions are already engaged. We want to make sure they stay that way. They can sometimes get taken for granted because they are so dependable as drivers of innovation. They may even end up getting burnt out because they do a lot of the heavy lifting in an environment that is metamorphosing into a future focused, agile, innovative workplace.

Our *Champions* are often our high performers. They can deliver 400% more productivity than an average performer![71] One of the keys to keeping them engaged is simply sitting down and talking with them – keeping them in the loop, discussing performance, giving good feedback.

Champions are like sponges when it comes to learning. They usually place a high priority on their development. A valued reward, therefore, is to support them to go on high-quality training as an addition to the self-directed learning they engage in for themselves. This is a way of demonstrating that you value their development as much as they do.

Keep them engaged also by showing them what they will learn from each new project. One high-performing millennial in China, who was ready to move on to another job, admitted that her boss's secret weapon for keeping her was "with every assignment she gives me, she also tells me what new thing I am going to learn by doing it."[72]

Global talent solution company Hudson produces a report each year about the key issues facing Australia's workforce. It reports that career progression (or lack thereof) and boredom can create "flight risks". "Employers who provide stretch assignments or secondments, and create clear, meaningful career plans, will be best placed to retain their top talent."[73]

Tips for Leaders

1. Make innovation "sexy" so that people want to come on board with new initiatives.

2. Encourage people to take breaks together, socialise together and have coffee and lunch together. Create a sense of community so people feel connected to each other.

3. Induct new employees properly from day one!

4. Make *employee experience* a priority. Good things will flow from this.

5. Engage people in different ways depending on their levels of skill and will.

In the Presence of Engagement ...

Knowledge is cultivated. People will be motivated to learn more.

Talent is developed. Because people are bringing their *whole* selves to work, they will be more passionate about what they are doing.

Experience is extended. People will often go above and beyond the call of duty when they feel valued and respected.

NOTES

EDUCATE

"Leadership and learning are indispensable to each other."
~ John F. Kennedy

CHAPTER 10

EDUCATE

"Education is the mother of leadership."
~ Wendell Lewis Wilkie

Now you can see why I chose those particular words with which to encapsulate the message about the seven meta-skills 21st-century leaders need to succeed in the innovation age.

Entrepreneurialism

Democratisation

Utilisation

Creativity

Adaptability

Thinking Strategically

Engagement

Those seven words give us the acronym **EDUCATE.**

Successful leadership in the innovation age requires us to be constantly educating ourselves, as well as encouraging and facilitating the ongoing education of our team members. It stands to reason that if leaders ask their people to step up and out of their comfort zones, they must ensure those team members are developing the skills to help them succeed.

Stepping out of the comfort zone can be very intimidating for people. If we are pushed too far out of our comfort zone to solve problems beyond our capacity, our endocrine system releases hormones that create a fight-or-flight response in the body. This, in turn, creates a state of anxiety and is physically discomforting. When this happens, we are operating in the panic zone, which is not enjoyable at all because people feel out of their depth. They feel as though they have been thrown into the deep end and can't swim.

So the message for leaders is to make learning enjoyable. Then people will *want* to go on the developmental journey and that will ultimately build the capacity of the organisation. Knowing how to do that is a great leadership skill.

That is not to say it is entirely up to the leader to provide all those opportunities. Rather, the importance of lifelong learning is taken as a given. Team members are encouraged to grow and challenge existing knowledge. The best way to do this is by example, by being the role model – by being a leader committed to constant learning and sharing your own learning journey.

Living in the Learning Zone

Good leaders who want to *develop* their people find a way of consistently *stretching* them by leading them out of their comfort zone into their *learning zone.* The learning zone is the place where people can:

- Develop new skills

- Gain fresh insights

• Acquire valuable experience

The actual name of this zone is *Zone of Proximal Development*, named after the great Russian psychologist Lev Vygotsky. He called it *зона ближайшего развития*. But we'll just call it the *learning zone*.

By asking good questions, good leaders prompt and nurture people to operate in their learning zone so they become lifelong learners. If you have an organisation populated with lifelong learners, good thinkers and good problem-solvers, by extension you have a learning organisation. That means you have an enterprise that will be innovative, responsive to change and able to meet the challenges of our complex globalised marketplace.

The leader's job today is to motivate and inspire people to *want* to live in the learning zone. American statesman John Quincy Adams said, "If your actions inspire others to dream more, *learn* more, do more and become more, you are a leader." Twenty-first century leadership is about teaching, mentoring and elevating rather than making decisions for or on behalf of others.

Leaders today are in the business of education – both their own and the people they lead. That doesn't mean being "the teacher" in a traditional sense, but creating the environment where people take responsibility for their own ongoing development; where people are nudged into using their knowledge in new ways, and encouraged to bring their insights from the latest TED Talk or industry conference to workplace challenges.

Is Success the Result of Raw Talent or Hard Work?

In her book *Mindset: The New Psychology of Success*[74], Stanford psychologist Carol Dweck, proposes a simple model for understanding why people are motivated differently when it comes to learning and, consequently, how this forms their attitudes towards new experiences. Dweck says people fall into two mindsets: a *fixed* mindset or a *growth* mindset. Her premise is that intelligence and talent are not set in concrete. Rather, we can become smarter and more talented depending on how we view the learning experience. It is a spin on Abraham Maslow's assertion that "in any given moment we have two options: to step forward into growth or to step back into safety."

Fixed mindset people believe success is the result of natural, raw talent. If you have to work too hard at something, you are not naturally gifted in that area. So someone who is trying to protect their identity of being considered smart and talented prefers to undertake activities they know they will succeed at. To do otherwise risks failure, which might expose deficiencies. They believe that if you are not born with a natural talent in an area, you could never master it.

A classic example of this is peoples' attitude towards maths. I have selected this example because, as I mentioned in Chapter 2, in my first incarnation (decades ago) I was a high-school maths and science teacher. If that point ever came up in conversation, it was not unusual for me to hear people say things like, "Oh, that was my worst subject in school. I'm just one of those people who can't do maths."

While I am only too aware that maths comes more easily to some than others, it's not that such people are completely incapable of it. It's just really hard! And I speak from experience. It was the subject in high school that I had to work the hardest at and which gave me the most angst, frustration and heartache – which is probably why I went on to teach it. I understood the struggle.

Growth mindset people believe their potential is unknown and that with effort and passion they will constantly improve. They view qualities such as intelligence and talent like muscles that can be strengthened with exercise. They see learning as a lifelong process.

Just to be clear, though – no amount of hard work in maths was ever going to turn me into an Einstein. But that's not what Dweck is claiming. Her message is simply that if we embrace challenge, persist in the face of setbacks and see effort as the path to mastery, then we are more likely to succeed. Whereas if we avoid challenges or feedback we don't like, get defensive when things don't work out or give up in the face of obstacles, then we are less likely to succeed.

In reality, of course, life is not black and white. We may have a growth mindset about some aspects of life and a fixed one about others. Even Dweck (post *Mindset*) has gone on to say that we are hybrids with different situations and challenges bringing out fixed or growth approaches. Nonetheless, Dweck's work helps to shine a light on our beliefs and prompts us to examine our attitudes towards difficult challenges. Even just being *aware* of the different mindsets can serve to shift our thinking.

It can all be summed up in one sentence. If we are afraid of failure, we won't try new things, thereby robbing ourselves of the opportunity to learn and develop. Leadership can be hard. The complex challenges we face in the workplace can be difficult and draining. And there is much that we can learn from them.

Here are a few practical suggestions about how you and your team can live in the learning zone.

Deliberately Create Learning Opportunities

Albert Einstein said, "I never teach my pupils. I only attempt to provide the conditions in which they can learn." Regularly set aside 15 to 20 minutes during staff meetings for some collaborative reflection, questioning and collective, creative problem solving.

Most challenges facing a team, department or organisation could be addressed using this simple approach and tapping into everyone's creative problem-solving skills.

Before consultations, mentoring or coaching sessions with emerging leaders, give them particular questions that will effectively focus their attention and reflection so that the discussion during the meeting is more productive and insightful.

Ask people to report on their *learnings* as well as their outcomes. Celebrate the learning and development *journey* as much as the results. And then help people make connections and links between how their elevated skills and experience can be applied to *other* workplace issues. In educational psychology-speak, this is referred to as transfer of learning – the ability to apply new knowledge to different contexts. The better we are at doing that, the better use we will make of our knowledge base.

When people operate in situations they find demanding and stressful, help them to realise that it is these same experiences that stretch them and develop their leadership skills. (Although, most of the time that is only appreciated in hindsight.) These are the experiences that help to create a body of knowledge and experience that will ensure they have a career that will serve them well. As Henry Ford said, "The only real security one can have in this world is a reserve of knowledge, experience and ability."

Reflection

Build a "reflection" component into *all* reporting (e.g., "What did you learn from this experience?"). So, when people deliver information about the outcomes of various projects at meetings or to executive committees, some part of that time is dedicated to articulating their own learning outcomes, as well as the project outcomes. Make sure it is an integrated expectation, not something that is tacked on. This will help them extract the learning and transfer it to other projects and help make them more adept at more complex assignments.

Value the strategic importance of thinking time by encouraging people to engage in some official uninterrupted "thinking time" at work, either in their usual space or in a specially purposed area.

Encourage teams to critically reflect on progress at specific times during a project by asking questions such as: What's working? What's not working? Are we using our resources wisely? What would we do differently from the beginning if we knew then what we know now?

Enculturating a workplace to adopt mindful, self-reflective practices takes time. But it reaps enormous rewards. Contemporary workplaces can become so busy that the emphasis on doing and taking action squeezes out the opportunity for thinking and taking stock. Yet the strategic importance of doing so is indisputable.

Questioning

Within any organisation, leaders who ask good questions will bring about a number of positive outcomes. They will:

- Encourage new ideas.

- Challenge unproductive mindsets.

- Prompt people into higher levels of thinking and problem solving.

- Help people acquire a more strategic and not just a tactical approach to their jobs.

- Create more self-reliant teams.

- Tap into people's vast store of unique knowledge, wisdom and experiences.

So adopting a "question-asking" approach is a sure-fire way to kick-start high-quality thinking and creative problem solving to generate innovation and harness a team's talent. Human evolution has been driven by asking good questions and then striving to answer them. Organisational evolution and sustainability depends on this as well.

Here are some questions to help nurture different kinds of thinking.

Questions that encourage strategic thinking:

What are your goals?

What outcomes do you want to achieve?

What are the best ways by which to achieve your objectives?

What initiatives have you started or stopped?

To what extent are short-term demands distracting you from your long-term goals?

Questions that encourage creative problem solving:

If I put this idea/concept/scenario/product into a completely different place or time, what would happen to it?

Can I blend two or more ideas together to create a new one?

What would happen if I did the opposite of what I should do?

What would I see if I examined this situation/idea from a completely different point of view?

What are the things I already know that I can use to get started with this project/problem/issue?

Questions that encourage reflection:

What made this project interesting/exciting/challenging?

How did you nurture your own professional development in this process?

What kind of help did you need for this project?

What did you learn?

What will you change or do differently next time?

Questions that encourage self-awareness:

How do you feel about this?

Why did this particular project challenge/excite/engage you?

What did you learn about yourself in this process?

How did you benefit from this experience?

Questions to encourage analysis:

What were the strengths and weaknesses of this approach or solution?

How is this a better or worse solution than the alternatives?

How could we have done this better?

Does this solution look like it will "deliver the goods"?

Questions that empower people:

What went really well?

What would you change if you had it to do over again?

What would you have done differently?

What did you learn from this experience that will change your professional practice?

Be a "Gadfly"

The term *gadfly* originated in ancient Athens. Its literal meaning is a fly that buzzes around and bites livestock – especially horses and cattle. In Greek mythology, the gadfly was used by Hera as the source of torment for Lo, a beautiful maiden turned into a heifer by Zeus to protect her from Hera's jealousies. (Bad plan. Not only was Lo now a heifer, she was also constantly tormented by horseflies.) From that story, the term gadfly came to be applied to people who constantly questioned and challenged the status quo, refused to accept popular wisdom and saw it as their civic duty to goad leaders out of complacency and force them to confront issues they would rather overlook.

Plato described Socrates as a gadfly because Socrates often got on politicians' nerves asking lots of questions – very often difficult ones that kept them on their toes. He was the original gadfly. Indeed, he was the father of the methodology of teaching and leading through questioning – called the Socratic method. This is where a good teacher or leader can help people to discover what they need to know – not by telling them but by guiding them to join the dots so they discover the answers themselves. The learning that comes from this is profound and meaningful.

Gadflies help prevent group think and encourage deeper levels of insight, reflection and analysis, all of which lead to better problem solving and decision making.

Create Communities of Practice

One of the greatest challenges for any organisation is how to access, develop, nurture, use and retain the knowledge that resides within it. Communities of practice are an easy way of encouraging knowledge sharing and informal peer mentoring. A CoP is simply a group of people who are empowered to learn from and with each other. CoPs provide the opportunity for people to extend as well as contribute their knowledge through collaboration.

Very often, people create their own informal communities within organisations. For example, a group of colleagues chatting in the lunchroom about how they handle difficult clients; frontline staff sharing their experiences while waiting at the bus stop; or a manager who sets up a yammer space for her team to exchange ideas between formal meetings. These are all examples of people networking and sharing knowledge. This can ultimately improve their workplace performance and productivity, generate new solutions and responses to challenges, and contribute to the collective knowledge base of an organisation. It actively involves members of the community in the teaching and learning process, and recognises that everyone can be a mentor with something to offer. And it can happen just as easily in a virtual environment as in a physical one.

If this informal process can be integrated into an organisation's processes, it has the potential to improve collaborative problem solving, facilitate the transfer of skills and knowledge across different sections of an organisation, enable the cross-fertilisation of ideas through people who may not otherwise have occasion to interact, and access the tacit knowledge resident within the organisation. Tacit knowledge is that huge body of information, experience and wisdom that defies capture through formal methods but is often imparted through shared activities.

In 2009, a group of employees (programmers) at technology firm Qualcomm found that they were thoroughly enjoying their lunchtime discussions about how to improve user experience. Soon the group started coming up with highly innovative ideas for solving problems that were forwarded to the company's patent committee. What's more, they were relishing the process and having fun. The first group spawned a second group, then a third.

Eventually, they formalised the process and named it the FLUX program. FLUX stands for Forward Looking User eXperience. This community of practice has replicated itself throughout the organisation internationally and has produced 60 patents.

CoPs can augment and deepen learning by making it a shared experience. Each quarter, I work with a small group of leaders in my *Innovative Leaders Mentoring Program*. Participants come from diverse contexts but they all have one thing in common: they are passionate about innovation. They see it as a vehicle for transformation and are committed to shaping an even better future for their workplaces and with their teams. The group goes on quite a journey together. To augment the face-to-face component of the program, we also inhabit for the duration of the program an online collaboration space where we share thoughts, expand learnings, gain additional insights, ask questions and offer different perspectives. This happens continuously and seamlessly and helps to create a shared immersive experience that brings remarkable results. The power of a CoP in action.

Access to Information – A Double-Edged Sword

The good news is it is easier than ever before to be educated – about anything. We have unlimited access to information 24/7. People can learn how to be social media experts, mathematicians, break dancers and even champion javelin throwers by watching YouTube or using any of the other multitude of online learning platforms. Julius Yego, who came eighth in the javelin finals of the 2012 London Olympics, had never had a formal lesson: he taught himself with YouTube! As did my daughter, who learnt the basics of playing the violin before she had her first lesson.

The flipside of this is we have so much information at our fingertips that we can become overwhelmed. The old saying "too much of a good thing is good for nothing" holds true here because not all information is created equal. Much of it is low-grade rubbish. In his book *Data Smog: Surviving the information glut*[75], David Shenk warns of the dangers of information excess, which can lead to chronic stress, high anxiety, ADD (attention deficit disorder) and a sense of fragmentation due to loss of context.

But then, that's part of the learning – developing an insight into knowing what is worthy of one's attention and what's not.

Yet even when we engage with high-quality information, there can be a downside. We can become passive *consumers* of information without taking the next step of looking for ways to apply it. We can watch TED Talks while exercising and listen to podcasts while driving. We can gorge ourselves on information without actively applying it. There is a term for this recent phenomenon of over-consuming information: infobesity! Nearly half of the office workers in the UK suffer from it and it is hurting their health and productivity.[76]

While it is wonderful to be able to watch or listen to leading thinkers share brilliant ideas in succinct blocks, it is also important to benefit from the experience by exercising that knowledge. Ask: "How can I use what I've just learnt from this TED Talk to solve XYZ issue at work?" "What does this story about someone's experience in another discipline, in another part of the world, in another context, teach me about leading my team more effectively?" "Can I learn vicariously from other leaders' experiences, which are so easily accessible and freely shared, to become a better leader in my own area?" Taking our engagement with content that one step further transforms us from consumers to creators.

Leadership in the Innovation Age

The innovation age requires leaders to think differently about how they bring out the best in themselves and their people.

The leader of the future is the leader who asks rather than tells, who mentors rather than directs, who requests rather demands, and who collaborates rather than commands. As with so many other shifts taking place today, there is a fundamental shift in what constitutes good leadership, i.e. the kind of leadership that brings out the best in people and creates a high-performing workplace. Let's conceptualise the evolution of leadership as follows:

Leadership 1.0: *"I'll tell you what to do."* This is the traditional style of authoritative **command and control** leadership, where the leader makes the decisions.

Leadership 2.0: *"I'll provide direction and trust you to do your job."* This is the leader who demonstrates confidence in their team members and **trusts** them to get things done without micro-managing them.

Leadership 3.0: *"I'll provide you with the opportunity, resources, context and space to develop yourself so you can perform at the highest level possible and I'll make myself available to mentor, guide and advise as needed."* This is the **supportive** leader who creates an environment in which innovation can flourish by tapping into the inherent talent of the team and actively supporting their development.

But even these distinctions don't tell the whole story. Because ultimately a good leader needs to be flexible enough to work across *all* styles. That is *Leadership 4.0!*

Leadership 4.0 has the *wisdom* to know *when* to be highly directive versus when to be a catalyst when to provide structure versus when to remove it, and when to mentor versus when to instruct. Giving a team member too much responsibility before they are ready for it, or before they have the skills to fulfil it effectively, can result in them going on stress leave. Conversely, not giving people opportunities to challenge and stretch themselves when they are ready for it can end up with them leaving. They'll find somewhere else more satisfying.

For this, leaders need "social intelligence". This is the ability to understand the situation, including the context and relationships. It is also the capacity to select an appropriate response and, ultimately, vary one's behaviour in response to changing conditions. The University of Phoenix's Institute for the Future produced a report identifying the top-10 skills needed for the workplace of 2020.[77] *Social intelligence* was identified as being number two on the list. Number one was *sense making* – the ability to determine the deeper meaning or significance of what is being expressed. In other words, understanding context through deep insights and intuition (something that artificial intelligence has trouble with).

To be a socially intelligent leader:

- Take the time to get to know your team members in a way that builds trust.

- Look for those subtle but important cues that signal unspoken needs.

- Be prepared to offer the tools, advice and the wise counsel of a mentor.

- Adapt your behaviour in response to changing workplace conditions, as well as changing needs of team members.

- Motivate team members and employees to have a burning desire to be outstanding.

The 4.0 leader says, *"I understand you and your context well enough to provide you with what you need to grow, develop and succeed."* The result is an engaged team that takes pride in its work.

The value of a 4.0 leader to an organisation is immeasurable. I believe yhe following table understates the impact – but I'm being conservative.

LEADERSHIP LEVEL	Leadership Style	Value to organisation
Leadership 4.0	Socially Intelligent	X 10
Leadership 3.0	Supportive	X 6
Leadership 2.0	Trusting	X 3
Leadership 1.0	Command and control	X 1

Table 3: Leadership style and value to the organisation

Leadership is a privilege. Leaders are given the opportunity to shape the future as well as to shape people's lives. They can either create or kill people's sense of purpose, meaning and significance at work. Today above all, people are looking for purpose in their work. The leader who can facilitate that will be successful in the workplace of the innovation age and will make good use of workplace knowledge, talent and experience to create a culture of innovation.

The wise leader of the innovation age will use the seven meta-skills of EDUCATE to maximise knowledge, unleash talent and leverage experience to create an innovative workplace. The table below sums up the value of applying these meta-skills.

LEADERS	META-SKILL	KNOWLEDGE	TALENT	EXPERIENCE
	ENTREPRENEURALISM	Valued	Harnessed	Amplified
	DEMOCRATISATION	Volunteered	Nurtured	Deepened
	UTILISATION	Activated	Flourishes	Tapped
	CREATIVITY	Synthesised	Optimised	Compounded
	ADAPTABILITY	Transformed	Expanded	Matured
	THINKING STRATEGICALLY	Recontextualised	Revitalised	Repurposed
	ENGAGEMENT	Cultivated	Developed	Extended
	T E A M M E M B E R S			

Table 4: Effect of leadership meta-skills on employee
knowledge, talent and experience

Imagine a workplace where the knowledge, talent and experience of its employees were strategically and deliberately channeled into identifying better ways of thinking and doing. It would be utterly transformative!

If you are a leader wanting to take your team on a transformative journey and help create a future-ready workplace that will thrive in the innovation age, here is a simple way of identifying what your strengths and opportunities may be. Do the questionnaire on the following pages, then create an action plan. Don't try to do everything at once – that's a surefire way of doing nothing. Start with a couple of areas where you feel you could get some quick wins and work outwards from that.

Organisations that want to thrive in the disrupted, exponential world of the innovation age need a critical mass of leaders who can live and lead by the principles of EDUCATE.

Table 5: Leadership Self-Assessment

To what extent do you do the following?	1. Not at all 2. A little 3. Sometimes 4. Often 5. Most of the time				
Think of entrepreneurialism as a new core skill for yourself and your team members.	1	2	3	4	5
Solve problems with an entrepreneurial mindset.	1	2	3	4	5
Look for the opportunities in failure.	1	2	3	4	5
Challenge the status quo in order to look for better ways of doing things.	1	2	3	4	5
Lead through influence rather than control.	1	2	3	4	5
Give others the opportunity to solve problems and guide and mentor as needed.	1	2	3	4	5
Involve others in decision making.	1	2	3	4	5
Take the time to get to know team members and find out what lights them up.	1	2	3	4	5
Encourage team members to get to know each other so they also have a sense of the knowledge, talent and experience that surrounds them.	1	2	3	4	5
Open the channels of communication to discover the extent of the capabilities resident in your team.	1	2	3	4	5
Believe that you and your team are capable of creativity.	1	2	3	4	5
Encourage your team to regularly use their creativity at work.	1	2	3	4	5
Deliberately use creative thinking tools to augment complex problem solving.	1	2	3	4	5

Consciously challenge your thinking and that of your team members about how you approach workplace problems to avoid becoming stuck in default mode.	1	2	3	4	5
Learn something new every day.	1	2	3	4	5
Look at situations from different perspectives.	1	2	3	4	5
Keep abreast of trends and megatrends that impact the work you and your team do.	1	2	3	4	5
Regularly engage in thinking and reflection time.	1	2	3	4	5
Consciously step out of operational mode and into strategic mode so you can give attention to the *important* and not just the urgent.	1	2	3	4	5
Help new employees or team members to feel welcome when they join the organisation or your team.	1	2	3	4	5
Actively create a sense of community so people feel connected with each other.	1	2	3	4	5
Make *employee experience* a priority.	1	2	3	4	5
Adapt your leadership style in response to the changing needs of team members.	1	2	3	4	5
Motivate team members and employees to have a burning desire to be outstanding.	1	2	3	4	5

ACTION PLAN

Short Term

_____

_____

_____

_____

Medium Term

_____

_____

_____

_____

Long Term

_____

_____

_____

_____

Tips for Leaders

1. Be an "EDUCATE-d" leader by applying the ideas and principles in this book.

2. Create the conditions where team members can learn and develop themselves.

3. Ask great questions that prompt people to think more deeply.

4. Be socially intelligent by discerning the particular needs of your team members.

5. Enjoy the privilege of leadership where you can create value in your organisation, as well as in the lives of team members.

In the Presence of the Principles of EDUCATE ...

Knowledge is maximised.

Talent is unleashed.

Experience is leveraged.

NOTES

NOTES

Continuing the Conversation

Scottish writer and historian Thomas Carlyle said, "The best effect of any book is that it excites the reader to self-activity."

This doesn't have to be the end. Come visit me at
www.drirenayashinshaw.com

If you are looking for:

- ways of creating a future-ready, vibrant, high-performing leadership team

- a process to take your organisation on an innovation journey or

- an experienced and inspirational keynote speaker and thought leader for your event

then you'll find information about that at my website.

I have created a suite of workshops, programs and resources dedicated to supporting your innovation needs and aspirations.

Alternatively email to admin@drirenayashinshaw.com or call +61 7 38495003.

I'd love to hear from you!

Cheers

Irena

"Dr Irena Yashin-Shaw assisted us to develop and sustain a culture of innovation in QCT. She has extensive knowledge and understanding of innovation and how to create an environment within an organisation for innovation to thrive. There were immediate benefits for our organisation from Dr Yashin-Shaw's work. They included enhanced communication and relationships across the organisation with much greater willingness of staff to contribute ideas and participate in making innovation happen; thinking differently about the challenges facing our organisation; increased confidence of staff in calculated risk taking; and an increased capacity of staff to use different tools and processes to develop options for innovative solutions. Processes were put in place to ensure the longevity of the program and that the innovation momentum is sustained. Participants of the workshops enjoyed Dr Yashin-Shaw's warm personality and her willingness to ensure their needs were met." *John Ryan. Director. Queensland College of Teachers*

"Irena is a powerhouse of energy and a driver of innovative thinking. I have been able to create an environment for my team that allows them to unlock their innovative ideas – ideas that they didn't know how to tap into. My team are inspired to try new things and to look for ideas in new and unexpected ways. I understand now how integral innovative thinking is to the future of how any organisation goes about its day-to-day business." *T. Young. Manager. DHPW.*

"Dr Irena Yashin-Shaw is one of the best in this space. She succinctly captures innovation and makes it 'real' to leaders. From small 'improvement' ideas to big-ticket items, Dr Yashin-Shaw takes participants through a range of tools, methodologies and concepts which are readily transferrable into the workplace." *Kristine Tully. Director. Business Development & Innovation. SmartService QLD.*

"We are now more strategic in our approach to innovation in our organisation. Consequently, we have adopted a more systematic, formalised and structured process for innovation, which has given us a good plank for future growth and progress. Our entire staff now helps drive innovation, which has resulted in more organisational depth and knowledge capture." *B. Cage. Managing Director. Trelleborg Engineered Systems.*

"In our department, innovation has been a hot topic for a while and I found Irena's content has really helped me to move some of my thinking about innovation into action. It has demystified innovation and given good ideas about how to create an innovative work place and build an innovative culture in my organisation." *T. O'Connor. Regional Director. Department of Communities. North Queensland Region.*

"Leading in a complex and constantly changing environment brings exciting, ongoing challenges. Irena's *Innovation Mentoring* provided very contemporary insights and skills to enable me to see where innovation is critical in this new world, and how we can be responsive and adaptable. Her program opened a creative thinking process which has flicked a switch on how I see, and use, innovation to energise us towards clever and smart workforces. Irena is certainly dynamic and very tuned into the needs of the individuals she works with. I found there were many times where the lightbulb came on. We were stretched to think critically as well as creatively about where we were personally and where our teams were at." *L. Smith. Director. Department of Health.*

REFERENCES

1. http://www.ceda.com.au/2015/06/16/five-million-Aussie-jobs-gone-in-10-to-15-years

2. Based on Buckminster Fuller's "Knowledge Doubling Curve"

3. Smart materials that transform over time. Check out MIT's Self-Assembly Lab. http://www.selfassemblylab.net/

4. Foster, R., & Kaplan, S. (2001). *Creative destruction: Why companies that are built to last underperform the market, and how to successfully transform them.* New York: Broadway Business.

5. http://www3.weforum.org/docs/WEF_Future_of_Jobs.pdf

6. https://www.ge.com/sites/default/files/Innovation_Overview.pdf

7. http://www.gereports.com/innovation-barometer-2016/

8. https://www.ted.com/talks/ken_robinson_says_schools_kill_creativity?language=en

9. Cialdini, R. B. (2007). *Influence: The Psychology of Persuasion.* New York: Collins.

10. Berger, R. (2009). *Innovating at the Top: How Global CEOs Drive Innovation for Growth and Profit.* Basingstoke: Palgrave Macmillan.

11. http://www.ddiworld.com/DDI/media/trend-research/global-leadership-forecast-2014-2015_tr_ddi.pdf?ext=.pdf

12. Hollingworth, P. (2016). *The Light and Fast Organisation: A New Way of Dealing with Uncertainty* (1st ed.). Melbourne, Australia: Wiley.

13. http://www.apsc.gov.au/__data/assets/pdf_file/0008/80000/Unlocking-potential-APS-workforce-management-review-Design_WEB.pdf

14. http://www.apsc.gov.au/publications-and-media/archive/publications-archive/empowering-change

15. http://www.psc.nsw.gov.au/reports---data/other-publications/ideas-at-work-review

16. https://innovation.govspace.gov.au/

17. Gahan, P., Adamovic, M., Bevitt, A., Harley, B., Healy, J., Olsen, J.E., Theilacker, M. 2016. *Leadership at Work: Do Australian leaders have what it takes?* Melbourne: Centre for Workplace Leadership, University of Melbourne. Available at: http://sal.workplaceleadership.com.au/

18. Gahan, P., Adamovic, M., Bevitt, A., Harley, B., Healy, J., Olsen, J.E., Theilacker, M. 2016. *Leadership at Work: Do Australian leaders have what

it takes? Melbourne: Centre for Workplace Leadership, University of Melbourne. Available at: http://sal.workplaceleadership.com.au/

19. Renko, M., El Tarabishy, A., Carsrud, A. L., & Brännback, M. (2013). Understanding and Measuring Entrepreneurial Leadership Style. *Journal of Small Business Management, 53*(1), 54-74. doi:10.1111/jsbm.12086

20. Barber, M. (2015). *How to Run a Government So that Citizens Benefit and Taxpayers Don't Go Crazy.* UK: Penguin Random House

21. Bason, C. (2010). *Leading Public Sector Innovation: Co-creating for a better society.* Bristol, UK: Policy Press.

22. https://www.ted.com/talks/haley_van_dyck_how_a_start_up_in_the_ white_house_is_changing_business_as_usual?language=en

23. http://www2.deloitte.com/content/dam/Deloitte/au/Documents/ Economics/deloitte-au-economics-digital-government-transformation-230715.pdf

24. http://www.pc.gov.au/research/completed/digital-disruption/digital-disruption-research-paper.pdf

25. http://www.news.com.au/finance/work/careers/thankyou-founder-daniel-flynn-shares-career-success-tips-with-chapter-one-book-launch/ news-story/a25835fba909cdd4655a891e36e879bc

26. Dowling, S. (2016). *Work with Me: How to get people to buy into your ideas.* Melbourne, Australia: Wiley.

27. Everett, K. (2011). *Designing The Networked Organization.* NY: Business Expert Press, LLC.

28. https://www.mosaicprojects.com.au/PDF/PMI-The-High-Cost-Low-Performance-The-Essential-Role-of-Communications.pdf

29. Collins, J. C. (2001). *Good to Great: Why Some Companies Make the Leap ... and Others Don't.* New York, NY: Harper Business.

30. http://au.hudson.com/portals/au/documents/hudson_report_h22016_ au.pdf

31. Columella. *De re rustica,* trans. H.B. Ash. London: William Heinemann, 1941.

32. http://www.mondragon-corporation.com/eng/

33. https://www.nceo.org/articles/research-employee-ownership-corporate-performance

34. Author of *The Rise of the Creative Class.* (Professor and head of the Martin Prosperity Institute at Rotman School of Management, University of Toronto)

35. https://public.dhe.ibm.com/common/ssi/ecm/gb/en/gbe03297usen/ GBE03297USEN.PDF

36. Dyer, J., Gregersen, H. B., & Christensen, C. M. (2011). *The Innovator's DNA: Mastering the Five Skills of Disruptive Innovators*. Boston, MA: Harvard Business Review Press.

37. Scott (1995). "Creative Employees: A Challenge to Managers." *Journal of Creative Behaviour*, 29, p. 64 – 71.

38. Plucker (1999). "Is the proof in the pudding? Reanalyses of Torrance's (1958 to Present) Longitudinal Data." *Creativity Research Journal*, 12. p103 – 114.

39. Frymire (2006) October 7. "The search for talent." *The Economist*, 8498, p11.

40. https://www.regent.edu/acad/global/publications/jsl/vol1iss1/JSL_Volume1_Issue1_2008.pdf

41. http://www.hpw.org.au/uploads/5/9/1/7/59177601/boedker_bogg_chong_meagher_mouritsen_2013_indicative_guidelines_final_december_6_2013.pdf

42. http://reports.weforum.org/future-of-jobs-2016/

43. Robinson, K., & Robinson, S. K. (2011). *Out of our minds: Learning to be creative* (2nd ed.). Oxford: Capstone Publishing.

44. West & Anderson (1996). "Innovation in Top Management Teams." *Journal of Applied Psychology*, 81, p 680 – 693.

45. Cleese co-founded the Monty Python comedy troupe.

46. https://hbr.org/2011/09/begin-to-think-differently

47. http://www.sciencemag.org/news/2002/03/monkey-see-cursor-do

48. Attributed to Richard Branson, but Steve Jobs also said, "Creativity is just connecting things."

49. Csikszentmihalyi, M. (1997). *Creativity: Flow and the psychology of discovery and invention*. New York: HarperCollins Publishers.

50. Berger, W. (2014). *A More Beautiful Question: The Power of Inquiry to Spark Breakthrough Ideas*. New York, NY, United States: Bloomsbury Publishing Plc.

51. https://hbr.org/2014/11/what-high-performers-want-at-work

52. https://www.worksafe.qld.gov.au/forms-and-resources

53. Kanter, R.M. (2011) "Zoom In, Zoom Out: The best leaders know when to focus in and when to pull back." *Harvard Business Review*. Page 2

54. Crowley, D. (2016). *Smart Work: How to Boost Your Productivity in 3 Easy Steps* (1st ed.). Brisbane, Australia: Wiley.

55. Pink, D.H. (2009). *Drive: The Surprising Truth About What Motivates Us*, New York, NY: Riverhead Books.

56. http://www.pestsmart.org.au/wp-content/uploads/2012/02/RABFS3_impacts.pdf

57. http://www.oecdobserver.org/news/fullstory.php/aid/3681/An_emerging_middle_class.html

58. https://hbr.org/2002/02/beware-the-busy-manager

59. It's my book – I can make up words.

60. Fox, J. (2016). *How to Lead a Quest: A handbook for pioneering executives.* Melbourne, Australia: Wiley.

61. http://time.com/3858309/attention-spans-goldfish/

62. The fabled Gordian Knot, which was in effect a knot of knots tightly entangled, is a story going back to 333BC Macedonia. It is now often used as a metaphor for a difficult or complex problem.

63. Volume 27, No. 5. September/October 2016.

64. http://www.forbes.com/sites/victorlipman/2013/09/23/surprising-disturbing-facts-from-the-mother-of-all-employee-engagement-surveys/#743bc8b41218

65. https://hbr.org/2014/11/half-of-employees-dont-feel-respected-by-their-bosses

66. Porath, C.L., Erez, A. (2009). "Overlooked but not untouched: How rudeness reduces onlookers' performance on routine and creative tasks." *Organizational Behavior and Human Decision Processes.* Vol 109, Issue 1. http://www.sciencedirect.com/science/article/pii/S0749597809000041

67. Shakespeare. *Richard III.* Act 1, Scene 1.

68. Keats, J. (1819). *To Autumn.*

69. Fitzgerald, F.S. (1925). *The Great Gatsby.*

70. Collins, J., 2005. *Good to great in the social sectors: a monograph to accompany good to great,* Boulder, CO: Jim Collins.

71. https://hbr.org/2014/11/what-high-performers-want-at-work

72. https://hbr.org/2014/11/what-high-performers-want-at-work

73. http://au.hudson.com/portals/au/documents/hudson_report_h22016_au.pdf

74. Dweck, C. (2008). *Mindset the new psychology of success: How we can learn to fulfil our potential.* New York, NY: Ballantine Books.

75. Shenk, D. (1997). *Data Smog: Surviving the information glut.* San Francisco, CA: Harper Edge.

76. http://news.microsoft.com/en-gb/nearly-half-of-the-uks-office-workers-are-suffering-from-infobesity-the-over-consumption-of-information/#sm.0000160u93tahlekfz9iuuswji305

77. http://www.iftf.org/uploads/media/SR-1382A_UPRI_future_work_skills_sm.pdf

INDEX